RAMBLES FROM DORSET TOWNS

(AND A COUPLE OF VILLAGES)

BY

EDWARD R GRIFFITHS

ANOTHER SET OF GUIDED WALKS
FOR AN INTIMATE EXPLORATION OF
THE BEST OF DORSET

INCLUDES HISTORICAL DETAILS OF PLACES VISITED

BOOK FIVE

BY THE SAME AUTHOR

THE STOUR VALLEY PATH   ISBN 0 9519376 1 8

"...the book is a gem which anybody...will add quickly and gratefully to their bookshelf" .....Dorset Life

THE CRANBORNE CHASE PATH   ISBN 0 9519376 2 6

"....combining exciting local colour with meticulous route information".....Greenlink Countryside Guide

"....the anecdotes and passionate descriptions will delight even those familiar with the Chase".....Western Gazette

THE BLACKMORE VALE PATH   ISBN 0 9519376 3 4

"....a walk to be savoured.   Happy rambling and enjoy Dorset".....Blackmore Vale Magazine

DORSET IN A FORTNIGHT   ISBN 0 9519376 4 2

"...reflects the diversity of landscape and beauty of the county....you won't be disappointed".....Country Walking

Long Burton Parish Church of St James the Great (South of Sherborne)

ISBN 0 9519376 5 0

Published by Green Fields Books
13 Dalewood Avenue, Bear Cross
Bournemouth, BH11 9NR

CONTENTS

LIST OF ILLUSTRATIONS

WALKS IN THIS BOOK

1 EASTON, PORTLAND

ROUTE 1 - 11.1/2 MILES - Generally easy, dry walking; clifftop paths and some undulating stony tracks through quarries. Dries quickly after rain.

ROUTE 2 - 7 MILES - As Route 1 but shorter.

ROUTE 3 - 5 MILES - As Route 1 but with less undulations.

2 STURMINSTER NORTH

ROUTE 1 - 10.1/4 MILES - Farmland paths, tracks and country lanes; level in river valley, some hills around Hinton St Mary. Can be a bit sticky underfoot after rain.

ROUTE 2 - 7 MILES - As Route 1 but misses Hinton St Mary.

3 SOUTH OF SHERBORNE

ROUTE 1 - 11.1/4 MILES - Initial hill path to plateau; then easy tracks, field paths and country lanes before downhill return. Dries out fairly fast, but sticky after rain.

ROUTE 2 - 8.3/4 MILES - As Route 1 but shorter.

ROUTE 3 - 8 MILES - As Route 1 but even shorter.

4 EASTBURY, CHETTLE AND FARNHAM

ROUTE 1 - 5.3/4 MILES - Level or gently sloping farm paths and tracks. Generally chalky - dries out well.

ROUTE 2 - 9.1/2 MILES - As Route 1 but extends into countryside and more gentle hills.

5 WINTERBORNE WONDERS

ROUTE 1 - 10.1/2 MILES - Some hills and high downs walking; ups and downs but long, level valley stretches as well (some on easy country lane). Valley soils can be muddy but tops are more chalky.

ROUTE 2 - 7.3/4 MILES - As Route 1 but without the valley walk.

6 SWANAGE AND PURBECK

ROUTE 1 - 11 MILES - Easy start; town, farm tracks and country lanes. Some steeper paths and tracks, up and down. Steep descent to Coast Path; undulations on return. Varies from clay to chalk, clay remains sticky after rain.

ROUTE 2 - 8 MILES - Ascent on road from town, then more level than Route 1 using Priests Way track. Same return as Route 1 from descent to Coast Path.

ROUTE 3 - 9.1/2 MILES - As Route 2 plus up/down extension into Langton Matravers.

ROUTE 4 - 9 MILES - As Route 1 but returning along Priests Way as Route 2. Avoids steep undulations on Coast Path.

1 EASTON, PORTLAND
2 STURMINSTER NORTH
3 SOUTH OF SHERBORNE
4 EASTBURY, CHETTLE AND FARNHAM
5 WINTERBORNE WONDERS
6 SWANAGE AND PURBECK

RAMBLES FROM DORSET TOWNS

INTRODUCTION

It is a truth universally acknowledged (Thank you, Jane Austen), that it is impossible to string two words together whilst listening to tapes of The Goon Show, so I have reluctantly switched them off in order to introduce my latest collection of really special walks through the lovely Dorset countryside.   Actually, it's strange how you come across secret places which aren't often visited and which are instantly recognisable as a fictional somewhere which you have held in your head for years. Apart from the surreal visions which are conjured up by their adventures, this isn't really anything to do with The Goons - It's just that I'm already rambling and it's only the first page.   No, what I mean can be illustrated by a wooden footbridge which we found near Stourhead on *The Stour Valley Path*.   This was just like the Poohsticks bridge in *The House at Pooh Corner* where Winnie the Pooh, Rabbit and Piglet were joined in their game by the floating Eeyore.   Similarly, certain groupings of trees and the odd thatched cottage can bring to mind a specific, sad or joyful, poem of William Barnes or snippets of *Lark Rise to Candleford* by Flora Thompson.   The 'pirates' graves at St Andrew's on Portland and the sweeping arc of Chesil Beach bring *Moonfleet* alive, especially when a rough sea pounds the shingle.   Perhaps this is what I have meant in the past when I have referred to the "magic of Dorset". It's a personal feeling and it will be different for everyone, but anyone with an eye for natural beauty could not fail to be stirred by the sights they will see on some of these new walks.   Still on literary connections, I am happy to report that I have found nowhere in Dorset so dead as the Trolls' forest in *The Hobbit*.   Sadly, the path from Scarth Gap to Pillar through the Ennerdale forest in The Lake District could have been the model for this desolate place.   No sunlight penetrates its thick, evergreen canopy, the floor is deeply strewn with dead pine needles and it is silent as the grave as you follow the gloomiest path imaginable.   It appears that this particular forest has been cited as all that is worst with the Forestry Commission and it will never be repeated anywhere else.   I can't wait for its eventual removal.   Bring back the birds!

Anyway, for all that is best about Dorset - England even - go out and sample this blend of fine whole day and half day rambles, which begin and end in an easily accessible Dorset town (alright, I admit it) - or village.   All are within the range of the average walker who enjoys an al fresco lunch, usually miles from any shops (*but, before you set out, make sure I haven't given any dire warnings of steep hills which may cause you a problem*)   If you load your backpack with just enough sandwiches and drinks to keep you fuelled until you get back - as well as your Ordnance Survey map, waterproofs and sun oil or extra jumpers (depending on which season you choose) - you'll be perfectly set for a beautiful, uplifting day out.   Each walk is different from any of its companions.   If one takes you up hills and down dales or along coastal paths (Look out for the Portland experience), the next may take you through farming land or along a river.   One may take you through small villages or to a market town, church or manor house whilst another may lead you over chalk downs or along wooded or ancient tracks.   Wherever you go, your spirits will soar in the clear, fresh air of Dorset's wonderful scenery and you, too, will find the 'magic'.

The maps are highly detailed (but without excessive and unnecessary note of adjacent gates this time), so you shouldn't have much trouble finding your way but, if you do happen to wander off anywhere, the relevant Ordnance Survey map which I advise for each walk will soon bring you back.

For the walks which do not begin in major towns, suitable Bus Nos are given. The most utilised are Wilts and Dorset and Southern National whilst many independent operators' timetables are listed in the booklets entitled "Public Transport in Rural Dorset" which are obtainable from Tourist Information Centres throughout Dorset. These timetables, which give full addresses of the operators, are also available direct from Dorset County Council, County Hall, Dorchester, DT1 1XT.

CIRCULAR WALKS IN THIS BOOK

Each walk begins with a description of the main features which you will meet during the day, together with the Map Reference for the starting point and the Ordnance Survey map/s which you should carry. For village departure points, parking areas - or any buses which will take you there - are included. There are Mileage Tables which will enable you to plan your journey and the highly detailed Stage Maps show you how far you have come from the start. Follow the Maps but don't miss the adjacent texts because that is where you'll find the extra details that will add to your enjoyment of the walks. As with *Dorset In A Fortnight*, I sometimes recommend that you stop walking to read the text but this is only when I'm concerned that you may walk over a cliff edge or miss a special view because your head is stuck in the book.

All of the groups of walks include a quick return alternative so that you can do a shorter circuit. However, if you find that you have the time, or suddenly feel that you can't bring yourself to go home yet, you can walk some more and be sure that it'll be just as enjoyable as the part that you have already walked - and completely different.

RIGHTS AND RESPONSIBILITIES

All of the Footpaths, Bridleways, tracks and lanes have been followed very carefully on these walks and there were very few problems just before the completion of this book - although a couple of planted fields had to be crossed where paths hadn't been reinstated are rerouted. However, if you should find a new obstruction on the correct route e.g. blocked, broken or wired-up gates or exits from fields, or lack of stiles, you should make a slight deviation and report the obstruction to the Rights of Way Section of Dorset County Council. Such obstructions are illegal under Section 137 of the Highways Act 1980.

If you come across a ploughed field and the route crosses it or follows the edge of it, the Path or Bridleway has to be reinstated within 14 days of ploughing to widths of 1m and 2m respectively for the cross-field ways and 1.5m or 2.5m respectively for edgewise ways under the Rights of Way Act 1990. If these reinstatements have not been made, cross the field or follow the edge as you wish, whichever is easiest.

If you find a gate open, leave it open but, if it's closed, close it behind you - and don't drop litter. Observance of these two simple requests is all that is required to make the relationship between hiker and farmer perfectly harmonious so, with the delights of the open country awaiting you, get ready to go out and enjoy yourself.

I know I don't really need to remind you but, as with all of the other books, I feel it behoves me to tell you that you will be visiting working areas of Dorset - not one gigantic theme park or recreation area. Then again, if you come across someone ploughing, harvesting, woodcutting, dry-stone wall building, foresting or sheep herding, they won't usually mind if you stop and watch for a while.

3

KEY TO MAP SYMBOLS

ROUTE

MILES FROM START

ADJOINING MAP NUMBER

FOOTPATH OR BRIDLEWAY ARROW

SIGNPOST

HEDGE

WIRE FENCE

WOOD/IRON FENCE

STONE/BRICK WALL

STILE

GATE - LARGE / SMALL

TREE - DECIDUOUS / PINE

SPECIFIC BUILDING

GROUP OF BUILDINGS (schematic)

TUMULUS/BARROW

STREAM/RIVER

BRIDGE OVER STREAM

CLIFF EDGE

GRADIENT (arrows point down)

OVERHEAD CABLES

Cave Hole and stone loading 'Whim'', Portland

Chesil Beach viewed from New Ground, Portland

PART ONE - EASTON AND PORTLAND

INTRODUCTION

The Isle and Royal Manor of Portland is only prevented from being a real island by a two-lane road sandwiched between a narrow strip of stony beach and a rough grassy ribbon.   Apart from that, this is a real island in the true sense of the word.   This is a foreign country.   The landscape and the people are unique and tourists miss all of the best bits by driving straight to Portland Bill, paying a fortune in the Car Park and then driving back to the mainland.   Known as "slingers" because of their ancient prowess with the sling-shot, Portland islanders live (frequently within their own private cloud whilst the rest of Dorset is bathed in sunshine) on solid rock with just a thin layer of overlying soil, unsuitable for growing crops but perfect for quarrying to satisfy the once-ravenous appetites of Government and Civic builders.   From the air, Portland is shaped rather like a pear-drop whilst, from the side, it looks like a door-stop as the limestone table dips from North to South - a distance of only 4 miles from its highest point of 496 ft to a mere 20 ft at its Southern tip.

The three walks show you all of the variety of scenery which this rocky island has to offer, with sheer cliffs and gentle grassy slopes overlooking Chesil Beach and Lyme Bay to the West and stone and grass clifftop paths on the East with views into some of the island's huge limestone quarries, fine views of Portland Harbour and the rugged coastline towards Purbeck.   You will see three lighthouses, ancient stone houses and fine churches, fossilised sea-shells in nearly every rock, a castle built by the son of William the Conqueror, an abandoned 13thC churchyard with skull and crossbones on hidden tombstones and, depending upon the season, colourful wild flowers and nesting seabirds.   This is a delightful island and exploration will be well rewarded.

THE ALTERNATIVES

I have chosen Easton Square (Reference SY692719 on OS Map No.194) as the best starting point as it is easily accessible, the buses stop here, there is a car park and there are many small shops.   Southern National No. 1 runs to Portland Bill from Weymouth at frequent intervals whilst open-topped buses are used in high summer.

ROUTE 1: Total distance 11.1/2 miles.   This Route goes straight to the West Cliff and passes the huge St George's Church and Blacknor Fort to bring you to the precipitous edge of the Coast Path.   Turning South, the path runs gently downhill for about 2.1/2 miles to Portland Bill with its stone ledges and a view of the tidal race. Turning along the East coast path, a clifftop walk leads past quarries and sheer cliffs which are home to nesting fulmars.   This Route visits the the 13thC St Andrew's church ruins and its tombs, Rufus Castle, H.M. Prisons (ancient and modern), 19thC gun batteries and wonderful viewpoints over Weymouth, Chesil Beach and the coast towards Devon before returning along exciting clifftop paths to Easton.

ROUTE 2: Total distance 7 miles.   This Route leaves Route 1 to complete its whole circuit of the Isle of Portland after you have seen St Andrew's ruins and passed Pennsylvania Castle, returning you to Easton along 1/2 mile of "Wakeham", a wide and fascinating road which is lined with old stone cottages.

ROUTE 3: Total distance 5.1/2 miles.   Beginning where Route 2 left off, this follows the second part of Route 1, around the North of Portland from Rufus Castle to the New Ground viewpoint and back to Easton along the towering West cliffs.

STAGE MILEAGES

STAGE	MILES	TOTAL MILES
ROUTE 1:		
1 Easton Square to Blacknor Fort	1	1
2 Blacknor Fort to Southwell	1	2
3 Southwell to Portland Bill	2	4
4 Portland Bill to Sheat Quarry	1.25	5.25
5 Sheat Quarry to Church Ope Cove	1	6.25
6 Church Ope Cove to Rufus Castle	.25	6.50
7 Rufus Castle to Broadcroft Quarry	1	7.50
8 Broadcroft Quarry to Waycroft Quarry	1	8.50
9 Waycroft Quarry to New Ground	1	9.50
10 New Ground to Easton Square	2	11.50
ROUTE 2:		
1 - 5 As Route 1 to Church Ope Cove	6.25	6.25
6 Church Ope Cove to Straits	.75	7
1 Straits to Easton Square	0	7
ROUTE 3:		
1 Easton Square to Straits	0	0
6 Straits to Rufus Castle	.50	.50
7 - 10 As Route 1 to Easton Square	5	5.50

Portland Bill - from Route 1 approach

EASTON AND PORTLAND ROUTE LAYOUT

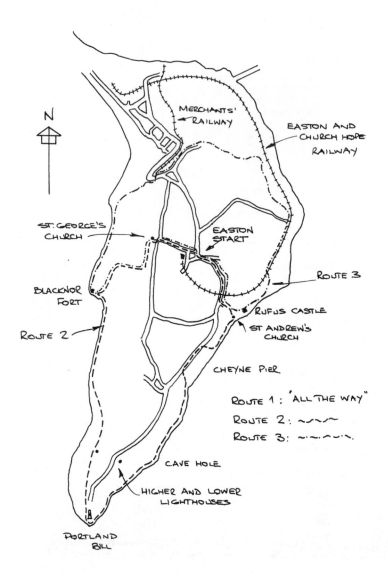

N

MERCHANTS' RAILWAY

EASTON AND CHURCH HOPE RAILWAY

ST. GEORGE'S CHURCH

EASTON START

ROUTE 3

BLACKNOR FORT

RUFUS CASTLE

ST ANDREW'S CHURCH

ROUTE 2

CHEYNE PIER

ROUTE 1 : 'ALL THE WAY"

ROUTE 2 : ~~~~

ROUTE 3 : ~·~·~·~·

CAVE HOLE

HIGHER AND LOWER LIGHTHOUSES

PORTLAND BILL

Clifftop Path at East Weare, Portland

Parish Church of St George, Easton, Portland

STAGE 1

EASTON SQUARE TO BLACKNOR FORT OR "STRAITS"

With a handy car park and the buses stopping here, Easton Square is the ideal starting point, mid-way between the East and West Coasts of the Isle of Portland.

ROUTE 1: Set off in a Westerly direction along the wide, stone house-lined street called "Reforne". After the Post Office on your left, you cross over the old railway line whose existence is recalled by the name of Station Road on the left. Passing various two and three-storeyed stone cottages, plus some later houses, this easy stroll continues, past the Y M C A, St George's Church Hall and Workshops on your right until you reach the cricket ground on the far RH corner of Reforne. Over on the left, at the end of the continuous row of old cottages, stands the Jacobean "George Inn", once the Parish Clerk's house and ancient site of the Court Leet. From here, continue to the end of the road and follow the wide verge around the stone-walled playing field and tennis courts on the left and then cross over the main road, with Wide Street turning off to "Weymouth A354" on your right.

The huge, cathedral-like church constructed of locally-quarried Portland stone facing you is the now-redundant Portland Parish Church of St George which was built in 1754-66 by Thomas Gilbert to replace the unstable 13thC Parish Church of St Andrew which you will see later at Church Ope Cove. The third in succession of these Parish Churches is All Saints which replaced St George's in 1917. You will pass this one as well, if you aren't doing the complete circuit in one go, on the return into Easton on Stage 2. St George's was one of the first churches to come into the care of the Redundant Churches Fund and the restored inside includes box pews and two pulpits - one for preaching and the other for conducting the services. The architect's grandfather was surveyor of the quarries when Christopher Wren was building St Paul's Cathedral in London so the resemblance between St George's tower and St Paul's West towers is probably more than coincidental.

Past St George's, follow the stone walls of the continuation cemeteries which contain many white, black and red marble tombstones whilst St George's houses 400 Portland stone tombstones and the local quarries are still supplying those simple, elegant headstones for the War Graves Commission. Anyway, past the Health Centre over on the left, turn onto the Footpath-signed track after the cemetery. There are playing fields down on the left and Bowers Quarry over the bank on your right. When the track turns left towards some blocks of flats and houses, keep following the bank into some common ground and then aim for the farthest end of the row of housing in a left diagonal direction. This brings you back onto the track as it bends around the housing estate between the ends of the rows of houses and a small allotment on your right. Follow the track, now an arrowed, gravel Footpath, between wire fences with small fields on either side. The RH gate at the end leads into a pony field and the path now zig-zags around the block wall of Blacknor Fort Stables. At the end of the path, a kissing-gate leads out of the LH field and you have reached the Portland Coast Path. The narrow path which turns off to descend on your right is the return from Route 1's complete circuit of the island but, avoiding the sheer drop of more than 400 feet into Lyme Bay, turn left and begin your grassy, slightly descending stroll to Portland Bill.

ROUTE 3: Set off past the pedestrian crossing in the far East corner into "Straits" with All Saints' Parish church just down on your left. Now, turn directly to Stage 6.

10

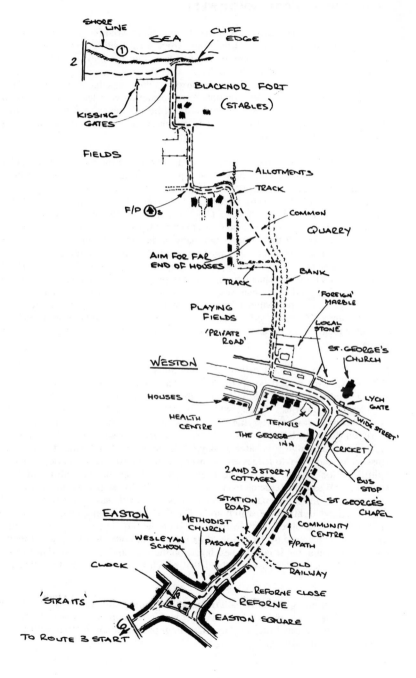

STAGE 2

BLACKNOR FORT TO SOUTHWELL

Settle down to a steady, easy walk with soft grass under your feet and wonderful views along the clifftops and out into Lyme Bay where local fishing boats and trawlers are working - but be aware that there is a terrible drop onto the rocks just feet away from your path for most of the next two miles. After the concrete gun-post just below the cliff top, the wide greensward begins to narrow as the cliff edge comes nearer and the wire fence of the blocks of Weston flats comes nearer on your left. Before you reach the end of the wire fence, there are old cliff-climbers' spikes near the edge although the modern climbers, of whom you will see many along this path, seem to manage without these old, rusty spikes.

The cliff face ahead of you gives an idea of the structure of the island - many layers of limestone with a thin blanket of soil on top. Although some of the best building stone in Britain has been taken from Portland (and most of the major buildings in London were built of Portland limestone), vast layers of unsuitable material had to be removed to get to the better stone. This accounts for some of the coastal scenery of Portland because most of the "spoil" was simply tipped over the edge of the cliffs - mostly in the North of the island. Not many of the landslips which you will see are natural - the limestone isn't really prone to slipping and the tumbling, rocky, coastal landscapes known as the East and West Weares of Portland are actually quarry tips. Weare is just a Portland name for a tip and this propensity for dumping over the edge has robbed Portland of its beaches. The only remaining bathing beach is that at Church Ope Cove and, whereas this was once a sandy beach, longshore drift has brought dumped pieces of stone along from the Weares, ground them into pebbles and deposited them on the beach. It is now a completely stony, although very popular, beach.

Now, continue past a short path which runs down to some startling rocky platforms and ignore all tracks and Footpaths which turn inland on your way around Portland. They will either take you into villages in the centre of Portland or, on the East coast, into dangerous quarries. Huge boulders are used to edge the fenced fields on your left as you keep on along the varying width tracks and, after an "East Cliff"-signed track joins you (from the left, of course), the less-used paths close to the cliff edge give the best views - although it is safer to stay on the more-used and wider tracks. More grass paths lead down to ledges and a lower path as you pass another track and a slight uphill section brings you to the high security fence of the redundant M O D Underwater Weapons Research Establishment. The lower path comes back up here and, when you reach the end of the security fence, you will have your first view of all three Portland lighthouses which are - The Old Lower Lighthouse which is now operated as a Bird Observatory by the R S P B on the left, The Old Higher Lighthouse which was once owned by Dr Marie Stopes, the birth control pioneer and founder of Portland Museum, but is now a guest house on the right and, barely visible to the left of the Old Higher Lighthouse, Portland Bill which replaced both of the other two in 1906

Now, keep on along the cliff path/track, still ignoring any turnings off, and pass between a huge rock and the Coast Path stone on the corner of a wire-fenced field. There are now various little, slightly ascending, paths to choose from with brambles between you and clifftop.

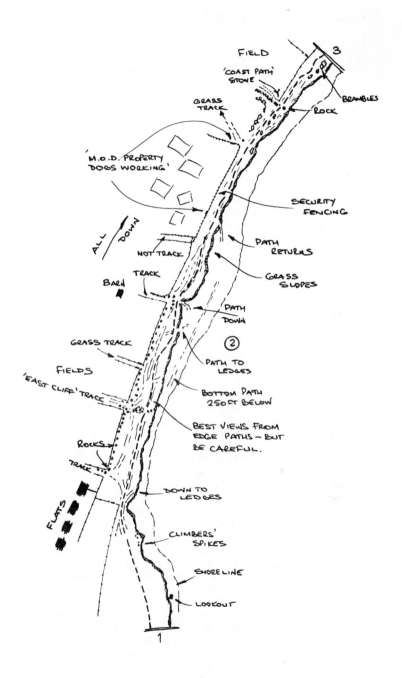

FIELD

'COAST PATH'
STONE

3

BRAMBLES

ROCK

GRASS
TRACK

'M.O.D. PROPERTY
DOGS WORKING'

SECURITY
FENCING

PATH
RETURNS

ALL DOWN

NOT TRACK

GRASS
SLOPES

TRACK

PATH
DOWN

BARN

②

GRASS TRACK

PATH TO
LEDGES

FIELDS

BOTTOM PATH
250 FT BELOW

'EAST CLIFF' TRACK

BEST VIEWS FROM
EDGE PATHS - BUT
BE CAREFUL.

ROCKS

TRACK

DOWN TO
LEDGES

FLATS

CLIMBERS'
SPIKES

SHORE LINE

LOOKOUT

1

13

STAGE 3

SOUTHWELL TO PORTLAND BILL

Passing along the bramble-edged track, you reach The Old Higher Lighthouse and, respecting the reason for the bank which has been constructed between the coast path and the painted walls of the lighthouse buildings, just keep on down, past another Coast Path stone and the fenced-in Coast Guard Lookout Station. A notice confirms that the LH track is "Private". Cross the tarmac lane which bends up to the CG Station and follow the one of many grass tracks which passes about 30 yards to the left of the three consecutive "High Voltage" aerial enclosures.

The stone building down on your left is the "Pulpit Inn" but it's not far to Portland Bill now and you can sit on the rocks and enjoy your sandwiches. Anyway, if you're going all the way round Portland, it will be quite early now. So, wend your way down along any of the grassy paths/tracks but generally aiming for the LH end of the next M O D security-fenced establishment down ahead of you. As you get nearer the establishment, many paths zig-zag through the brambles and you should now aim for the RH edge of the un-enclosed, but rock-marked car park. This angle should get you across the similarly rock-edged, tarmac lane which runs to the M O D front gate exactly at a Public Footpath arrow-post. In this corner of the car park, you will see the bus stop for the Southern National No. 1 which runs (open-topped in the summer) almost every 15 minutes to Weymouth , via Easton Square.

However, follow the RH side of the car park down to the Public Conveniences before continuing South, past the Portland Bill Lighthouse, across the wheelchair path which leads to a stone-walled viewpoint, and to the ledges beyond the triangular obelisk which was erected by Trinity House. That's what the "T.H." stands for - but, for many years, I thought it was a memorial to one of the Thomas Hardys, either the writer/poet or Nelsons flag captain. Actually, on a clear day, you can see the Admiral Hardy monument high up on an inland ridge behind the far end of Chesil Beach.

Standing on the ledges behind the monument, you are on the lowest point of the Isle of Portland's limestone table top at approx. 20 ft above sea level, on the Southernmost tip of Dorset with France being the next land mass, and with the notorious "race" where the tides of Weymouth Bay and Lyme Bay meet above the limestone shelf dipping away in front of you. This rough junction of fast currents causes many problems for small craft and there is an apocryphal tale of a small yacht attempting to sail from Poole to Lyme Regis which reached here alright, spent three days trying to beat the speed of the "race" but eventually gave up and went back to Poole. The Lighthouse behind you was built between 1903 and 1906. It stands 136 ft high and has foundations 7 ft deep - and this on a base of solid Portland stone.

Now it's time to follow the coast path along the East side of Portland so turn away from the obelisk and follow the grassy, rocky paths/tracks with a collection of gaily-painted wooden Takeaways and tea shops on your left. Various fishermens' huts near to the stone-loading hoist, known as a "whim", have been joined by a sprawling shanty town of beach huts whilst the boulder-edged track soon leads past a barrier and a "Crown Estates" sign on a rock cube as another track comes down from the road on your left. The various stone-walled enclosures are all that remain of the attempt by the Dorset War Agricultural Committee to farm the shallow soil in a medieval strip system during the last war. Keep straight on and pass through a gap in the stone wall in front of you with more huts on your right.

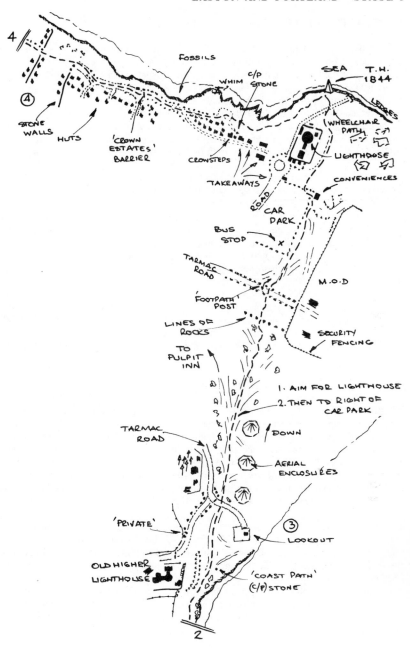

4

FOSSILS

c/p STONE

WHIM STONE

SEA T.H. 1844

LEDGES

④

STONE WALLS

HUTS

'CROWN ESTATES' BARRIER

CROWSTEPS

WHEELCHAIR PATH

LIGHTHOUSE

CONVENIENCES

TAKEAWAYS

ROAD

CAR PARK

BUS STOP

TARMAC ROAD

M.O.D

'FOOTPATH' POST

LINES OF ROCKS

SECURITY FENCING

TO PULPIT INN

1. AIM FOR LIGHTHOUSE
2. THEN TO RIGHT OF CAR PARK

TARMAC ROAD

DOWN

AERIAL ENCLOSURES

'PRIVATE'

③ LOOKOUT

OLD HIGHER LIGHTHOUSE

'COAST PATH' (C/P) STONE

2

15

STAGE 4

PORTLAND BILL TO SHEAT QUARRY

After a half-circle of huts on your left, keep following the path which is joined by other tracks from the stone wall-bordered huts on your left. Go around the chains on either side of the track from the main road up on your left, with a grassy shelf down on your right. There is just one last bunch of huts and then the path skirts around a small cove and follows the cliff edge around the right edge of a field. A path has been walked directly across this field to the crane (whim) but the real Footpath keeps to the edge. Approaching the whim, you will see a vast cave underneath it. It goes quite a way back into the cliff and you will have to peer very hard to see into it. This is Cave Hole, a monument to the strength of the Portland stone which forms its roof.

Now, with a small quarry on your left, before a wire fence, follow the row of small stone cubes across the wide greensward with loose rocks scattered about right and left. This will lead you to a railed footbridge over a small stream which runs across the hedged field and disappears over the cliff edge on your right. Across the next open, grassy area, there are some huts and a working crane down on the ledges. This denotes the start of a walk through a completely different environment to any which you may have previously encountered anywhere in Dorset - away from the easy, grassy paths and onto much stonier, undulating paths. As the Isle of Portland dips from North to South, it follows that there will be more useful layers of stone above sea level the further North you go. From the next track on your left, which runs down to the huts on your right and also turns to lead you Northwards past a Footpath-arrowed boulder, much of the stone between the cliffs on your left and the seaward cliff has been removed. The unusable stone has been back-filled into the quarries or tipped over the cliffs to form a low-level environment of rock and rubble nearer the sea.

So now begins your lunar landscape stroll - and I have heard that some of the early Doctor Who episodes were filmed in these quarry remains. Up and over the first rise, the path leads to cast concrete bases of some long-gone Sheat Quarry equipment before a high square boulder wall. My guess is that these bases were for vast cranes which could reach back to the quarry cliff and swing out over the sea. Here is where back-filled stone leaves a canyon before the quarry cliff over on your left but, being such vast blocks, the top layer of stones, grit and soil can suddenly slip down into the voids between them and great care should be taken if you choose to explore. Now, duly warned, continue along the rising path, passing around mounds of spoil and scattered boulders with holes of varying sizes before the cliff face on your left.

The limestone strata has, or had, vast, deep cracks running for hundreds of yards across its otherwise smooth and level surface. These varied in width from a few inches to 2 ft and thousands of years of surface water running into these cracks formed limescale patterns on the sides - something like curtains of thin stalactites. As quarrying removed the stone, these cracks were often used as the boundaries for the quarry and, as you walk along these paths, you will see the limescale coating on the cliffs as they become higher and more sheer over on your left. Now weathered, you will still be able to make out the flattish formations of smooth, brown-shaded stalactite material.

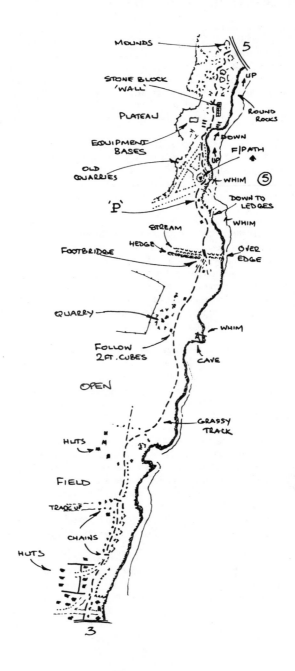

STAGE 5

SHEAT QUARRY TO CHURCH OPE COVE

Up the path, with holes, spoil mounds and rocks scattered around, a track goes off to your left just before a limescaled cliff face.   Now level, now descending, there is a ravine over on your left and then, after a grassy ascent, a Coast Path stone points up the next track to West Cliffs.   At a wider section of level track with protecting boulders along the steep RH cliff drop, the LH cliff face is used as a training ground for budding climbers.   Don't be tempted to join in - not today, anyway.   Keep on along the steeper, rough and stony path, now between clumps of brambles, past a track which leads to a ledge on your right overlooking Freshwater Bay.

Go around the barrier at the top of the track, past the "Public Footpath" arrow, onto a junction with the "Private" signed track which leads to Cheyne House over on your right, near the cliff edge.   Unlike some of the less stable sea cliffs in Dorset, this position is perfectly secure - away from the eroding element of the waves, at least. You will remember Cave Hole and how secure was its relatively thin roof.

Carefully cross over Portland Bill Road to the opposite pavement and turn right, passing the weighbridge house of Suckthumb Quarry over the low stone wall.   After the wide entrance to the quarry, where a Footpath arrow points uninvitingly into its depths, the low stone wall which follows your pavement appears to have been built by an amateur or a somewhat inebriated professional.   You have about 1/2 mile of pavement before you can turn back to the seaward path again but, after the stone-walled paddock on the other side of the road, the scrub has been cut back to form a wide, grassy verge which will be kinder to your feet.   If you use it, watch out for the cars coming in and out of the Viewpoint at Cheyne Weares.

Another Footpath sign points into the broken-walled fields on your left and, soon after this, there is a stone seat built into the more abstinent builder's length of wall. Leave the main road to go on its way to Portland Museum and, ultimately, Easton and turn down the signed, bramble and scrub-bordered Footpath on the right.   Follow its zig-zag past Dunecroft (disused) Quarry to continue with more cliffs on your left and the sea on your right.

There is a secondary path through the rocky foreland nearer to the sea but stay on the main path.   You can see Rufus Castle from here, ahead of you, but I'll tell you more when you get there.   Down the cut steps between boulders, the path soon opens onto a wider patch with rocks below you.   There are scattered boulders all around, many with yellow painted Footpath arrows, as the path meanders, past a square stone block wall on your right and up some rock steps.   At the top of these, don't take the less-used first path but the next one which is joined by another path apparently emanating from the cliffs below the ranks of caravans lined up on the edge above you.

Go up some more rock steps and then zig-zag down again - minding your head on the huge boulder which shadows the next descending steps - and then passing a large, cuboid stone on your right.   The stony beach which lies ahead is Church Ope Cove - Portland's only true holiday beach.   I mentioned before that this was once a sandy beach but the many years of quarry dumping to the South has resulted in ground stone being transported along the coast by longshore drift and being dumped here as rounded pebbles.

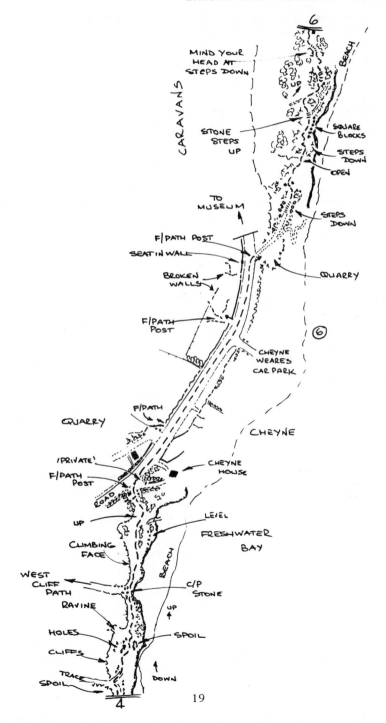

6

MIND YOUR
HEAD AT
STEPS DOWN

BEACH

UP

CARAVANS

STONE
STEPS
UP

SQUARE
BLOCKS

STEPS
DOWN

OPEN

TO
MUSEUM

STEPS
DOWN

F/PATH POST

SEAT IN WALL

QUARRY

BROKEN
WALLS

F/PATH
POST

⑥

CHEYNE
WEARES
CAR PARK

F/PATH

QUARRY

CHEYNE

'PRIVATE'

CHEYNE
HOUSE

F/PATH
POST

ROAD

UP

LEVEL

FRESHWATER
BAY

CLIMBING
FACE

BEACH

WEST
CLIFF
PATH

C/P
STONE

RAVINE

UP

HOLES

SPOIL

CLIFFS

TRACE

DOWN

SPOIL

4

19

STAGE 6

CHURCH OPE COVE TO RUFUS CASTLE AND STRAITS
plus STRAITS TO RUFUS CASTLE

Down the long run of steps between bushes and trees and behind beach huts, you arrive at a tarmac path with sets of steps which lead down from Rufus Castle to the beach. What was that? Trees? On Portland? Well this *was* part of the Pennsylvania Castle estate and the unusual decorative trees and shrubs were specially planted here. Now, go up the tarmac path, past turnings into the beach huts' gardens. After the sharp left bend, the path continues on a sharp right bend to Rufus Castle, confirmed by the Coast Path sign for West Cliff. Don't follow it but take the minor, stepped, path signed for "13thC Church (Ruins)". At the top of the wall-and-handrail enclosed steps, you emerge onto a walled viewpoint which is actually part of the abandoned 15thC churchyard of the Isle of Portland's parish church of St Andrew. The sign said 13thC but the now ruined building is of about 1450, standing on the site of the original Saxon church which was destroyed by Danish raids in 787 and 837AD. The great weight of the building required continuous stabilising and maintenance and, in 1753, the costs forced the parishioners to abandon this church altogether and to build another, larger and even more grand, parish church on the other side of Easton - St George's which you have seen already. Before you leave the churchyard, have a look in the bushy, low left corner (on the seaward side) and you will find two casket shaped tombs. One of them is dated 1699 and carries the skull and crossbones adopted by pirates. There are others but *I* haven't found them yet.

Leaving through the pointed stone arch outside the South end of the church ruins, follow the long ascending, sometimes stepped, path through the "woods" with a lovely layered garden beyond the fence on your right. At the top, join the tarmac track with a high stone wall facing you and turn left. Follow the path round to the right, still upwards and between stone walls, where the track goes through a wooden gate into the grounds of Pennsylvania Castle - a vast, castellated stone house, now converted into select flats. Begun in 1797, this fine country home was built by James Wyatt for the Governor of Portland, John Penn, grandson of the founder of Pennsylvania. It was officially opened in 1800 by Elizabeth, daughter of George III who was a frequent visitor to the area.

Emerge onto the pavement of Pennsylvania Road, with Perryfield Quarry entrance and Church Ope car park opposite, and turn right, along a buttressed stone wall to the old entrance gateway of Pennsylvania Castle - now separated from it by several houses and their driveways. The road which turns down to your right, past Portland Museum, is Church Ope Road and it leads to Rufus Castle and the continuation of Route 1.

ROUTE 1: If you're going all the way, turn down here, past the Museum and turn to Stage 7. I'll tell you more about the Museum on that Stage - There's more room.

ROUTE 2: If you're stopping now and going directly to Easton, turn up Wakeham and follow the long, wide road as shown on this Stage map, all the way to the top and bear left, along the street called Straits, back to Easton Square.

ROUTE 3: Past the somewhat continental shady pavement on your right, continue along Straits and bear right into Wakeham. Follow the 1/4 mile long, wide road down to Portland Museum and the Church Ope Road turning, signposted for "Rufus Castle". Now turn to Stage 7 to continue and for more information about the Museum.

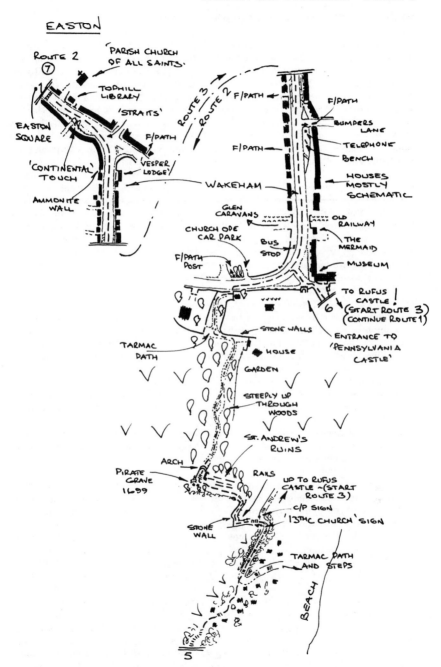

EASTON

ROUTE 2 ⑦

PARISH CHURCH OF ALL SAINTS

TOPHILL LIBRARY

'STRAITS'

EASTON SQUARE

F/PATH

'CONTINENTAL' TOUCH

VESPER LODGE

AMMONITE WALL

ROUTE 3

ROUTE 2

F/PATH

F/PATH

F/PATH

BUMPERS LANE

TELEPHONE

BENCH

HOUSES MOSTLY SCHEMATIC

WAKEHAM

GLEN CARAVANS

OLD RAILWAY

CHURCH OPE CAR PARK

BUS STOP

THE MERMAID

MUSEUM

F/PATH POST

TO RUFUS CASTLE !
(START ROUTE 3)
(CONTINUE ROUTE 1)

STONE WALLS

ENTRANCE TO 'PENNSYLVANIA CASTLE'

TARMAC PATH

HOUSE

GARDEN

STEEPLY UP THROUGH WOODS

St. ANDREW'S RUINS

ARCH

PIRATE GRAVE 1699

RAILS

UP TO RUFUS CASTLE ~ (START ROUTE 3)

C/P SIGN

'13TH C CHURCH' SIGN

STONE WALL

TARMAC PATH AND STEPS

BEACH

5

21

STAGE 7

RUFUS CASTLE TO BROADCROFT QUARRY

ROUTES 1 and 3: You should all be heading down Church Ope Road now, with the high walls of Pennsylvania Castle on your right and various houses, including Bow and Arrow Cottages, on your left. Before you disappear around the left bend, let me tell you more about the Portland Museum which you have just passed - or visited. The Museum consists of two thatched cottages, Number 217 Wakeham and the adjacent 1640 cottage which was made famous as Avice's cottage in Thomas Hardy's novel "The Well-Beloved". The buildings were donated to the people of Portland by Dr Marie Stopes, late owner of the Old Higher Lighthouse and pioneer of birth control. They were restored and opened as a Museum in 1932 and, due to an ever-increasing array of exhibits, the rear extension was added in 1973.

Keep on down, past the LH Tea-Shop and the walled house on your right, and pass around the edge of the barrier. Pass under the mock Norman arch which John Penn added to Rufus (or Bow and Arrow) Castle. The castle was probably built by William Rufus (reigned 1087-1100), son of William the Conqueror, and has Portland stone walls (what else?) 7 ft thick. It is in a pentagon shape with many loopholes for bow and arrow defence. In 1142, the castle was taken from King Stephen by Robert, Earl of Gloucester, for his mother the Empress Maud. After that, Richard, Duke of York seized Portland and, finally, George III gave the castle to John Penn.

Below the castle, you arrive on a wide, grassy viewpoint with steps and a tarmac path descending to Church Ope Cove. Yes, Route 1 walkers, I admit it. These would have brought you straight here from the beach huts - but you would have missed St Andrew's church, Pennsylvania Castle and the Museum. Pass the plaque and the Footpath sign and ascend through brambles and bushes. Some long, stone steps bring you, past a mound on your right, to a banked and levelled gravel track which carried the old railway line from Easton station to Weymouth. Bear right onto the track - but only for about 30 yards - unless you want to take an easy walk on the lower level and clamber back up a very steep path when you reach the M O D Firing Ranges.

LOW LEVEL: On this path, you'll soon see fulmars nesting in the cliff faces if it's the right time of year so keep going, past the LH intersection, with steep cliffs above you and the boulder-strewn Weares on your right. We'll meet again on Stage 8.

HIGH LEVEL: If you're taking the high road with me, go up the bank's stony ramp and follow the steep, bending path, with some wood-reinforced steps, up to the clifftop where you join a quarry track. Turn right and go past the instant right, downward track. Follow the worn grassy path up and along the line of rusted steel posts near the cliff edge, after which you pass a yellow-arrowed marker stone. Ignoring all of the tracks from disused quarries on your left, pass a couple of spoil mounds and masses of scattered rocks as your path wanders quite near to the cliff edge at times. *Note: There are several yards of path between all of these specific points.*

You have good views along the Lulworth coast, past Worbarrow Bay towards St Aldhelm's Head as you progress whilst the dour looking buildings ahead of you, slightly left, are the Napoleonic prison which is now used as a Young Offenders Institution. Keep ignoring left tracks and, after a few squared boulders cross your path (a yellow arrow painted on one), keep straight on between a brick building and a row of iron railings although a fenced path veers left to go around Broadcroft Quarry.

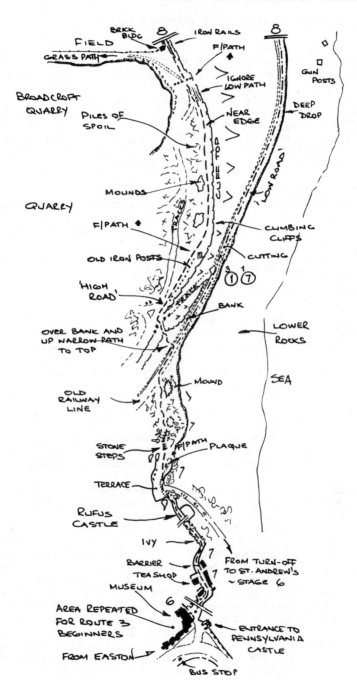

STAGE 8

BROADCROFT QUARRY TO WAYCROFT QUARRY

LOW LEVEL: I said it would be uphill on the way back to Easton didn't I?   It isn't on this track - but the cliffs on your left, where the fulmars nest in summer, are getting much higher and you have to climb the path to the top in a few minutes. Now you can see the reason for the embankment because it disappears as the cliff face comes nearer, not far from a concrete lookout post on your left.   It's covering large diameter soil/waste water pipes and, just after the "M O D Property. Firing Range. Keep Out" warning notice, it is joined by another from Grove Cliff and the Borstal buildings atop the cliffs.   The conjoined contents are then discharged somewhere out to sea on your right.   It must be alright, though.   The water at Church Ope Cove was declared the cleanest in the U K after a survey in 1994.

When you reach a "Cliff Falls" notice and steps down to Folly Pier on your right, turn over the pipeline to find the winding Footpath to the top of the cliffs.   (If you reach concrete steps up to a second concrete lookout box, you've gone too far).   Climb this path until you reach the road outside Grove Farm Borstal and join everybody else.

HIGH LEVEL: Passing between the bank on your left and the iron fence/stone wall on the cliff edge on your right, you soon reach a West Cliff and Coast Path stone near to the kissing gate leading into the field behind the bank.   I will not give many details regarding the buildings which you are about to pass but I will guide you safely round them.   The path now runs between low stone walls with lawns, trees and a bowling green over the LH wall.   As it bears away from you, this wall is replaced by an iron fenced cottage garden and, in your pathway, there are two stones - one Dorset Coast Path Number 8 and the other bearing an anchor insignia and the Number 74.

You now emerge, past a stone 'chimney' with grills half way up (which I take to be ventilators from waste water pipes below the ground), into a wider area with parking on your left.   Follow the road up past the car park with high fence-enclosed units on your right.   The road meets The Grove on your left at a T-junction whilst, next to a Footpath sign and directions to East Cliff and Church Ope Cove, there are two elevated viewpoints either side of a fenced section overlooking the cliffs and East Weare.   Keep straight on, passing Grove Farm Borstal and past two Footpath signs where the Low Levellers come up to join in.   Sorry it's not very scenic just here.

All together now!   Follow the long road with the low, winding stone wall along the cliff top and round to the left when a high stone wall blocks your route.   Follow this wall to a gateway which leads into an open, stony and grassy plateau.   Another road comes up from your left and skirts around the stone-walled enclosure on the other side.   It then disappears downhill after passing the two stone buildings in front of you and another viewpoint beyond these.   Follow the track which crosses the road on a right/left zig zag, keeping the long stone wall on your left.   A Footpath sign confirms your direction which leads through some large stone blocks across the track.   Portland Harbour and Weymouth are clear in the direction of the disappearing road.   When your track divides and the LH track runs down into Waycroft Quarry, past old "Danger. Blasting" signs, bear right and keep the high spoil bank on your left. When you reach a small cliff at the end of this bank, the track runs straight on into the quarry but you should take the right turn again.   Follow this track on a zig zag between two mounds to follow another LH bank which guards the edge of the quarry whilst the area opens out into scrub and scattered rocks on your right.

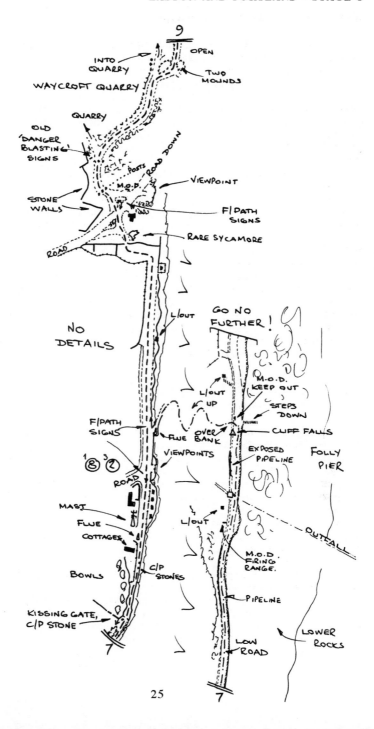

STAGE 9

WAYCROFT QUARRY TO NEW GROUND

At the end of this bank, where another track turns into the quarry, a Footpath arrow points along a wire fence-enclosed yard of The Verne Prison towards East Cliff. *Do not go through the barrier onto the gravel track on the other side* but turn left through the boulder barricade to keep the quarry bank on your near left.

If you feel like exploring, the foundations, excavations and underground arsenal of High Angle Battery are submerged over on your right - but be careful, there are steep drops into the 'alley ways'.   The modern Verne Prison buildings are mainly hidden by the grass embankments of the old citadel which was built during construction of Portland Naval Base, commenced in 1847.   Incidentally, the current Borstal which you passed earlier is housed in the prison buildings which accommodated the convict labour employed to build the Naval Base.

Follow the embankment around a right-sweeping bend past rough steps up the bank on your left and up to the High Angle Battery on your right.   Passing a RH wide gulley, you will find yourself in a strangely silent, high banked ravine.   Follow this until you reach an old concrete base on your left, then turn up the path to the road and emerge at a Footpath arrow and another anchor insignia (No. 22) where your gulley runs under the road.   Turn left on the road and, over another bridge, join the wood-fenced tourist path on the right as it runs along the edge of New Ground, overlooking Fortuneswell and Chesil Beach on its sweep North-West to West Bay.   On your way along this gravel path, you pass two angled paths leading down the steep slopes whilst the green over on your left is much used for kite-flying and family games. The old Merchants' Railway track ran along the slopes just below this viewpoint and the early 1880s stone bridges which you may have seen crossed the old tramroads which led from the quarry grounds to this Railway.   Before the construction of the Merchants' Railway, stone was mainly let down to the piers by sleds controlled by teams of horses or counter-balancing blocks of stone.   The incline, which ran all the way to the present Portland Base quay in Castletown, survived until 1939.

When the tourist path runs out, keep following the road, past the left turn to the Toilet block before Portland Heights Hotel and past the descending right Footpath to Fortuneswell at the "New Ground" sign.   If you want to go back to Easton, it's only 3/4 mile straight on past the Toilet block but you'll miss the most wonderful clifftop walk.   So, keep to the road and walk past the two paths which lead to the cenotaph and the steps up to the group of benches against the stone wall on your right.   After the lumps of fossilised wood in Portland Heights 'garden' and as the road bends left into Yeates Road, turn right down the narrower tarmac lane with a motorway-type crash barrier on its steep side.   After 50 yards, go through the barrier onto a descending footpath with a RH handrail.

On arrival at the New Road pavement, walk up the hill for about 100 yards and, before the sweeping bend of Priory Corner, cross over to the RH side where the path heads towards the cliff top.   Go through an opening in the low stone wall by the "Coast Path" sign and begin your cliff walk, passing a stone seat perched on the cliff edge on your right and the first of many "ravines' which lead through grassed spoil heaps into successive quarries on your left.   Continue along the path, passing the single stone seat in the ravine entrance to Tout Quarry.

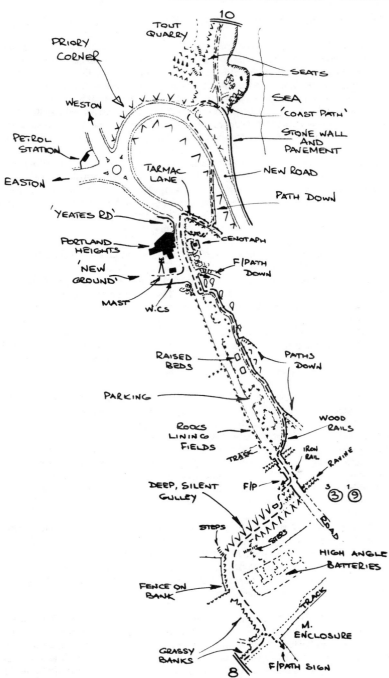

STAGE 10

NEW GROUND TO EASTON SQUARE

Being quite tired by now, take great care along this cliff path even though there are many strategically placed stone blocks to assist your avoidance of vertical plunges. Overall, this path leads downwards as you have finished with the highest point of the Isle which, at 496 ft, was just up the road from New Ground towards Easton. On your left, there are innumerable canyons or ravines running through the ancient, grassed-over spoil heaps which run between your path and the quarries behind them. Don't look too intently down these canyons whilst walking because there are sheer drops to the rocks below, very close to the RH edge of the path.

On the way, you have fine views of the trawlers and fishing boats down below you in West Bay and extensive views along Chesil Beach in the normally hazy direction of Lyme Regis and the Devon coast. Looking back towards Portland Harbour and Weymouth, the cliffs appear most dramatic but I recommend that you stop before looking. Sorry I'm going on about taking care but I feel somewhat responsible for your situation (not legally, I hasten to add, only morally).

After a squeeze through a pair of huge rocks and an up-and-down path before a sheer drop over the cliff edge, you go between two specially constructed piles of squared boulders which once supported overhead tracks for the "dumping" trolleys as they crossed over the Merchants Railway lines. The path then widens, rises and falls with the main track soon running into Trade Quarries. Bear right off the track and keep following the line of the cliffs on the Coast Path. This is confirmed by a marker stone at the next left path for East Cliff. After holes to left and right and another grassy path coming from your left, a path comes up from the RH ledges. Here, you will see deep grooves in the base rock where the Merchants Railway tracks ran along these cliff edges on their way up to New Ground.

As you begin to descend, you will see a complete squared-stone rock arch ahead of you on the edge of the vast cliff. Approaching it, there is a terrible drop on your right but, after the rock arch, the distance between the path and the edge becomes much wider whilst there are more canyons through the spoil on your left. Opposite the third canyon, there is a specially placed rock on the edge of the path where there is yet another sheer drop and, after that, the path hugs the spoil heaps well away from the two-levelled edge. There are now green slopes below you and, after a long grass gulley on your left, a rock table and a spoil mound on your right, you pass one last canyon before a gun emplacement base on a wide platform beloved of cliff climbers.

With huge blocks of stone projecting from the hill on your left, climb the stone steps to meet an indistinct path coming from your left alongside a banked wire fence. The fence leads along your path to a banked concrete block wall. On the upward, narrowing path, this forces your path extremely close to the edge of the cliff. I had to pass somebody on the narrowest part and he, ungallantly I thought, leaned over the bank and I had to go nearer the edge.

Well, you made it! At the end of the block wall, you come onto a wider, grassy, more level path. This is Blacknor Fort where you first came upon the Coast Path after your walk from Easton. I have repeated some of Route 1 on this Stage map but, after you've followed it to St George's church, I'm sure you'll be able to find your way back to the Square. If in doubt, turn to Stage 1 map again for the directions along Reforne.

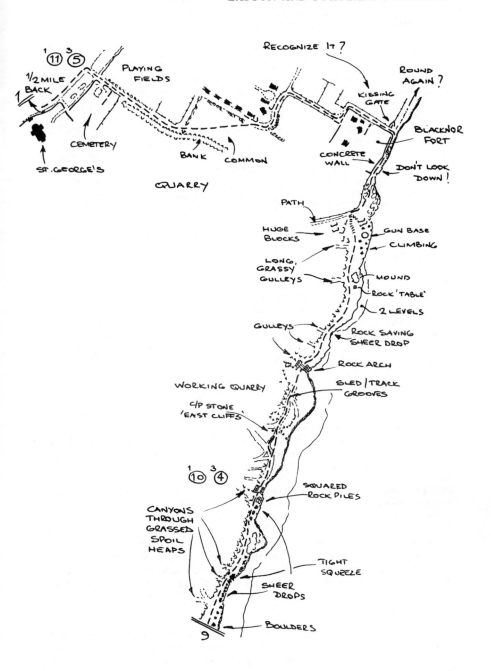

RECOGNIZE IT?

ROUND
AGAIN?

KISSING
GATE

BLACKNOR
FORT

① ③
⑪ ⑤

PLAYING
FIELDS

½ MILE
BACK

CEMETERY

BANK   COMMON

CONCRETE
WALL

DON'T LOOK
DOWN!

ST. GEORGE'S

QUARRY

PATH

HUGE
BLOCKS

GUN BASE

CLIMBING

LONG,
GRASSY
GULLEYS

MOUND

ROCK 'TABLE'

2 LEVELS

GULLEYS

ROCK SAVING
SHEER DROP

ROCK ARCH

WORKING QUARRY

SLED/TRACK
GROOVES

C/P STONE
'EAST CLIFFS'

① ③
⑩ ④

SQUARED
ROCK PILES

CANYONS
THROUGH
GRASSED
SPOIL
HEAPS

TIGHT
SQUEEZE

SHEER
DROPS

9

BOULDERS

PART TWO - STURMINSTER NORTH

INTRODUCTION

Being mostly in river valley farmland, these walks are relatively easy and level but, for the same reasons, you should be prepared for some mud after periods of rain. Our base for these walks is the market town of Sturminster Newton which has long figured in the farming history of Dorset and still holds weekly cattle markets. At the same time, being just a few miles from the birthplace of William Barnes, Dorset's greatest poet, and being the town where he gained his first employment, Sturminster Newton carries the air of a town of literary importance as well. Barnes has walked where you will walk on your meanderings around this lush dairy land and his wonderful dialect poetry reflects the scenes which you will still find and the people who you will still meet in this peaceful, enduring Dorset landscape. If you pop into Candy's black-timbered shop in the Market Place, you will find all that you could possibly need for your journey, together with a copy of Barnes' works to remind you of the spirit of *Stour Minster/New Town* when you have gone back home. I have visited this area many times, during the preparation of *The Stour Valley Path* and *The Blackmore Vale Path* and sometimes just to enjoy the pastoral spirit of this beautiful corner of Dorset.

THE ALTERNATIVES

Starting and finishing in Market Place, close to but not outside "The Swan Inn" (after all, these aren't Pub Walks) - at Reference ST787142 on O S Map No. 194 - you visit Sturminster Mill and cross the River Stour at Colber Bridge to join the old Stalbridge to Sturminster Halter Path. You pass close by William Barnes' birthplace at Bagber Common but as his home was registered as building number seven, its exact location is still disputed - clearly saving it from the exploitation suffered by the houses of other great writers and poets such as Thomas Hardy and William Wordsworth. Every summer, Hardy's Cottage at Higher Bockhampton is thronged with visitors from all over the world whilst Wordsworth's many homes in Cumbria have almost become small American states. However, I digress (again). Easy farm and field walking brings you to Cutt Mill and then the path divides into Routes 1 and 2, leading the quick-return walkers directly back to Sturminster Newton along the Stour whilst the rest visit the lovely village of Hinton St Mary with its neat church and Manor House - home to several personages of renown or of mystery - and Manston, enjoying a longer sojourn in the Vale of the Little Dairies.

ROUTE 1: Total distance 10.1/4 miles. You begin with an easy stroll out of town and along the edge of the River Stour to Sturminster Mill. Crossing the Stour over Colber Bridge, you join the old Stalbridge to Sturminster Mill Halter Path which you follow to Bagber. You then follow farm tracks and bridleways to Cutt Mill where water lilies grow above the weir. Then, tracks and field paths lead to Hinton St Mary where you can visit St Peter's church and the Manor House. Now, with fine views all round including to Shaftesbury, Hambledon Hill and Okeford Hill, you tread farm paths to Manston and follow the Stour back to Sturminster - passing the Old School where William Barnes held a teaching post opposite Mr Dashwood's old office - and visit St Mary's church.

ROUTE 2: Total distance 7 miles. This Route reduces the length of your walk by bringing you back to Sturminster directly from Cutt Mill along the River Stour. This way, you will enjoy a fine riverside stroll which is a relatively new creation, not shown on older O S maps.

STAGE MILEAGES

STAGE	MILES	TOTAL MILES

ROUTE 1:

1 Market Place to Colber Bridge	1.25	1.25
2 Colber Bridge to Bagber	1.25	2.50
3 Bagber to Cutt Mill	1.50	4
4 Cutt Mill to Hinton St Mary	1	5
5 Hinton St Mary to Home Farm	1	6
6 Home Farm to Manston	1.25	7.25
7 Manston to Stour Fields	1.25	8.50
8 Stour Fields to Rixon	1	9.50
9 Rixon to Market Place	.75	10.25

ROUTE 2:

1 - 3 As Route 1 to Cutt Mill	4	4
4 Cutt Mill to Stour Bend	1.25	5.25
...and onward, along the edge of the Stour to join the Colber Bridge path on Stage 1 from Sturminster Newton and back into Market Place	1.75	7

Manor House, Hinton St Mary

31

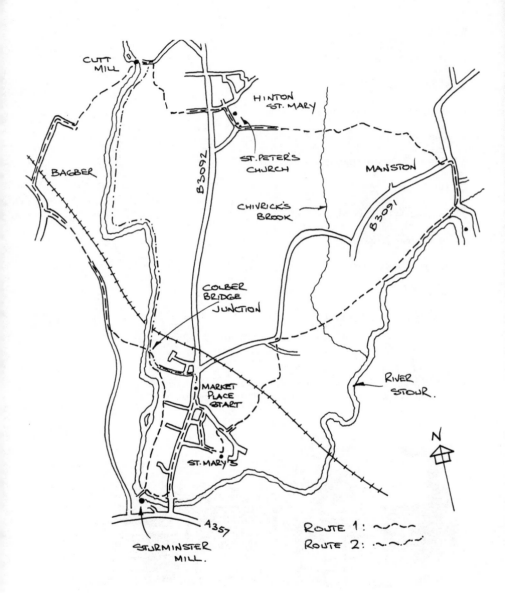

CUTT MILL

HINTON ST. MARY

ST. PETER'S CHURCH

BAGBER

B3092

MANSTON

CHIVRICK'S BROOK

B3091

COLBER BRIDGE JUNCTION

RIVER STOUR.

MARKET PLACE START

N

ST. MARY'S

A357

STURMINSTER MILL.

ROUTE 1: ~~~~
ROUTE 2: ·~·~·~

Sturminster Mill

Colber Bridge, Sturminster Newton

33

STAGE 1

MARKET PLACE TO COLBER BRIDGE AND RIVER STOUR TO TOWN

Sturminster Newton proclaims itself the capital of the Blackmore Vale - with some justification as it holds the weekly market and it is bigger and more strategically placed than its rival, Stalbridge. *Stour Minster* with St Mary's church stands on this side of the 10-arched bridge across the Stour, facing *New Town* with the scant remains of a castle mound on the other side. Both of these Walks pass the mill but only Route 2 actually passes the church, so I'll tell you more about them at the right time.

ROUTE 1: After Candy's, follow the main road, past the 1703 "White Hart" which stands opposite the remains of Sturminster town cross, and cross Ricketts Lane. The raised pavement on your left leads into Church Lane and to St Mary's. Downhill now, go past a couple of parking spaces and the fine stone "Beech House" over on your left and past a small factory and "The Cottage" on your right. Cross Durrant and follow the pavement with a low field on your right and with a gate and kissing gate onto a riverside path in the deep hedge on your left. A thin wood marks the end of the RH field just opposite the traffic lights and, as you begin to walk over the land arches which were added to the bridge in 1825, you will see Sturminster Mill over on your right. Go through the kissing gate into the meadow and follow the signed path along the fenced River Stour, over two drainage channels, towards the mill.

Most of the mill is late 17thC and, on the main door jamb, you can see flood levels of 1756 and 1979. In exceptional winters, the River has been known to freeze over so thickly that ox-roasts and skating have been enjoyed here, notably in 1882, 1895, 1933 and 1963. At the end of the fence, where the signed path from "Colber Bridge 1/2" comes down the field on your right, you can go through the kissing gate to visit the Mill. Returning, follow the direction of the "Colber Bridge 1/2" signpost, heading up the field to a gate which you will see midway between the single, tall Victorian house in the trees and the LH end of these trees. Go through the kissing gate into the War Memorial Recreation Ground with its superb specimen trees.

Cross the field through the trees, with the River Stour below on your left, and go through the next kissing gate where you will see the targeted Victorian house on the RH corner. Go down the path through a newly-planted wood, signed for "Colber Bridge 1/4", ignoring branches off to right and left. You should be aiming at the RH arch of the partly demolished rail bridge, passing close by an old, corrugated iron boat house. Climb over the Footpath-arrowed stile in the hedged fence facing you and turn instantly left to go over a second stile. On the other side, a signpost points straight on for "Stalbridge Lane 1/4 and Road Lane Farm 2.1/2". Cross a tractor track and ignore any side paths as you follow the LH hedge to the white painted iron Colber Bridge with a huge willow on its LH side. There was "anciently a manor or hamlet, now only a parcel of ground that still retains the name. *Colesberie* in the Domesday book could be this place": Rev Hutchins - but the O S definitive map places medieval Colber farmstead over the hedge on the other side of Stalbridge Lane. Cross over the bridge and the stile on the other side where another signpost points straight on to "Stalbridge Lane 1/4" whilst, after just 100 yards, Road Lane Farm is a whole mile nearer. Walk diagonally right across the field towards the junction of farm gates, ignoring the track which runs left to the farm gate in the facing hedge.

ROUTE 2: Still following the River Stour, go under the railway arch and, when you find the Colber Bridge path which you met earlier, turn left and return to Market Place

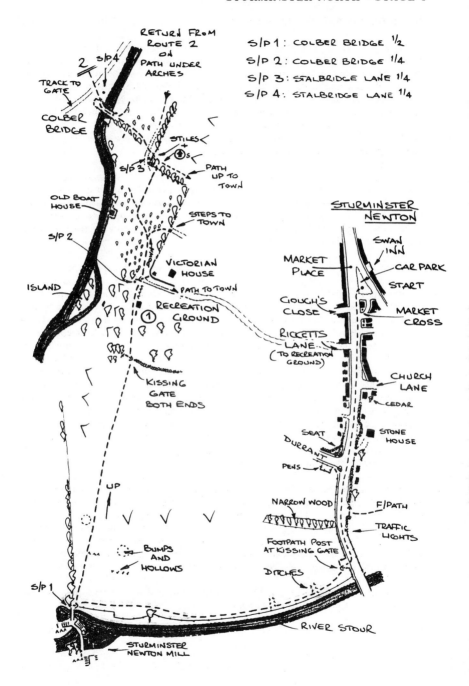

S/P 1 : COLBER BRIDGE ½
S/P 2 : COLBER BRIDGE ¼
S/P 3 : STALBRIDGE LANE ¼
S/P 4 : STALBRIDGE LANE ¼

RETURN FROM ROUTE 2 ON PATH UNDER ARCHES

2 S/P 4

TRACK TO GATE

COLBER BRIDGE

STILES

S/P 3

PATH UP TO TOWN

OLD BOAT HOUSE

STEPS TO TOWN

S/P 2

VICTORIAN HOUSE

ISLAND

PATH TO TOWN

① RECREATION GROUND

KISSING GATE BOTH ENDS

UP

BUMPS AND HOLLOWS

S/P 1

STURMINSTER NEWTON MILL

RIVER STOUR

STURMINSTER NEWTON

SWAN INN

MARKET PLACE

CAR PARK

START

CLOUGH'S CLOSE

MARKET CROSS

RICKETTS LANE (TO RECREATION GROUND)

CHURCH LANE

CEDAR

SEAT DURRANT

STONE HOUSE

PENS

NARROW WOOD

F/PATH

TRAFFIC LIGHTS

FOOTPATH POST AT KISSING GATE

DITCHES

35

STAGE 2

COLBER BRIDGE TO BAGBER

Arriving at the field gates junction, go over the Footpath-arrowed stile into the next field. Immediately, ignore the clearer path which runs right to Colber Farm buildings but keep straight on, close to the LH hedge and leylandii trees, and drop down to the gate and stile which lead out onto the tarmac of Stalbridge Lane. This high-banked and hedged Halter Path is the old Stalbridge to Sturminster Mill road along which horses and carts were led to and from the mill, exchanging corn for ground flour. In fact, a Halter Path is one along which you may lead a horse but not ride it. The site of Colber medieval farmstead is over the hedge facing you at the stile - but there are no visible signs any more.

Turn right and walk up the lane in the direction of "Bagber 1". 80 yards after a high LH oak, you will reach a junction with a cattle grid on your left and a drive leading to Colber Farm on your right. A Footpath to "Pleak House Farm 3/4" turns off left before the barns but keep straight on, past the RH farmhouse and LH leylandiis, to a gated area of barns on your left. The tarmac runs out here and the track becomes narrower, uphill, between high banks.

After the brow of the hill, you drop down to Blackwater Bridge where willows and beeches pleasantly overhang the water lilies (or clotes, as William Barnes calls them) of the River Divelish as it prepares to join the Stour. After the bridge, keep straight on past an area of gates where the track becomes a mere path between high-banked hedges. After twin iron posts which block the passage of unauthorised vehicles or carts, you may find scattered remnants of the ancient cobbled stone road surface along the 1/4 mile of the narrow Halter Path beneath your feet.

Leaving the confined path at a clearing with gates either side, the track becomes wider and continues upwards amongst some sycamores and oaks until, past the top of the slope, you descend to a LH bend with a track turning off right by some shady oaks. Now, more steeply upwards on rough and broken tarmac, you pass under an overhanging sycamore and two oaks, after which there is a gate on your right from where a good view of Hinton St Mary can be obtained. Then a deep verge with deep trees on your left is instantly followed by high banks on either side as you begin to descend towards the Manor House, Bagber.

Young William Barnes would have known this fine stone house with its high garden walls and slate roof. He would have gazed through the ball-topped gate pillars as you will do as you pass. The registration of his birth in March 1801 only gives his place of birth as Number 7, Bagber but many of the smaller farm cottages of the hamlet have long since disappeared. His daughter, Lucy Baxter, recalled that William was born on a farm called Rushay and there still exists a farmhouse of this name, just off the drove to Bagber Common.

Continue past the Manor House drive with the stone and brick barns, past the "No Through Road" sign and past the "Halter Path" sign.

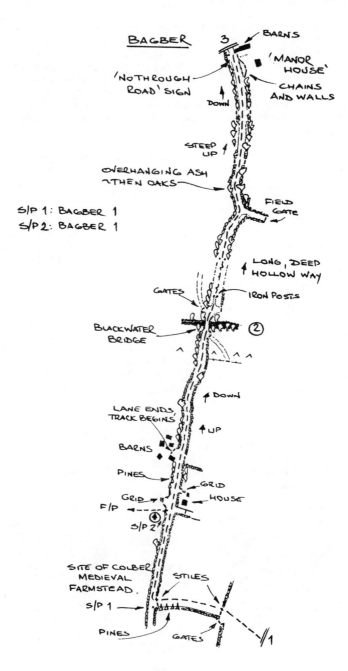

BAGBER

3

BARNS

'MANOR HOUSE'

'NO THROUGH ROAD' SIGN

CHAINS AND WALLS

DOWN

STEEP UP

OVERHANGING ASH ~ THEN OAKS

FIELD GATE

S/P 1: BAGBER 1
S/P 2: BAGBER 1

LONG, DEEP HOLLOW WAY

GATES

IRON POSTS

BLACKWATER BRIDGE

②

DOWN

LANE ENDS, TRACK BEGINS

UP

BARNS

PINES

GRID

GRID

HOUSE

F/P

④

S/P 2

SITE OF COLBER MEDIEVAL FARMSTEAD.

STILES

S/P 1

PINES

GATES

1

STAGE 3

BAGBER TO CUTT MILL

With the postbox on the triangle facing you, there is a useful bench round to your left if you feel like a rest.   Then follow the lane straight on, past cottages on the left and high hedges on the right.   Around the sweeping bend, turn first right at the "Bagber House Farm" sign.   Walk uphill, bearing right, past the fine stone farmhouse and its ancillary outbuildings on your left and past some red brick cottages, after which verges of varying widths alternate from side to side along the high-hedged, long and level lane.   After another 1/4 mile along this lane, a track turns off left on a bend as you reach the LH red brick and RH grey brick parapets of the old, badly cracked, pre-Beeching railway bridge.

After the bridge, the lane bends sharp right and then continues past a LH concrete farm track and the wood fence on stone walled garden of Lower Bagber Farm.   Here, the lane narrows and grass grows up the middle as the lane becomes confined between high hedges.   Shortly, you reach the cattle-gridded entrance to a red brick cottage on your left, after which a Bridleway sign points left into the grassy barnyard of Pentridge Farm as the lane keeps straight on over another cattle grid.   Go through the half gate next to the two big gates into the yard and keep straight on across it, along the cottage garden hedge.   Now, go through the facing gate with the "No Cyclists" label, between the RH wire-fenced field and the LH high hedge (with fragrant dog roses in early summer), onto a wide and grassy track which descends slightly around a sweeping right bend.

At the end of the track, go through one of a pair of gates, with a Bridleway arrow, and enter a wide field which descends slightly.   Follow the RH hedge, past a gate and a cattle trough, to the bottom RH corner where another gate leads into another wide and level field in the Stour Valley bottom with views towards Sturminster Newton and Okeford Hill on your right.   Keep straight on along the right edge of the wide ditch with the wire fence on its other side, listening to the chorus of bird song from the nearing wood and the water song from the approaching Cutt Mill weirs.

Cutt Mill

38

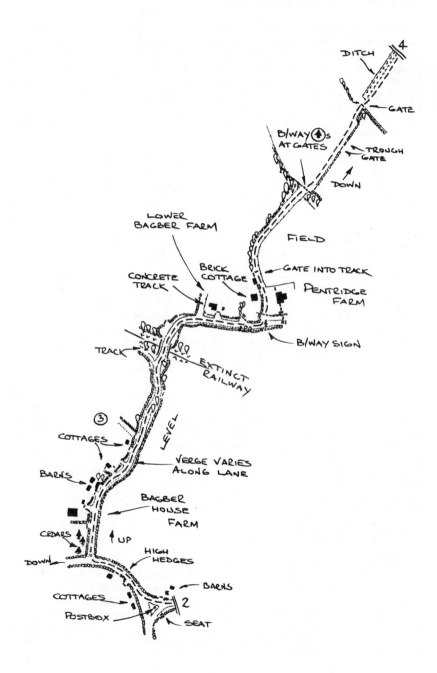

STAGE 4

CUTT MILL TO HINTON ST MARY

At the end of the ditch, turn left over the unusual stile and slatted bridge into the adjoining field.   Turn instantly right and go through the old half-gate onto the walkway between the LH mill pond and the RH, tree-edged lily pond.   Go over the concrete-surfaced Stour bridge and the wood-surfaced mill race bridge from where you can see the remnants of Armfield and Co., Ringwood's water wheel.   Have a good look around and then continue up the lane straight ahead, past the "Bagber 1" signpost on the corner pointing back the way you came.   Over the RH hedge, there is a lovely thatched cottage with pink roses around the door and a lawned garden which runs alongside the Stour.   Idyllic.

However, keep on up the hill with the new trees planted in the LH bank as the lane bends round to the right.   Here, you have to decide whether to go straight back to Sturminster Newton along the riverside on Route 2 or keep on to see Hinton St Mary, Manston and St Mary's church on your approach into Sturminster Newton - enjoying more of the Vale of the Little Dairies on Route 1.

ROUTE 1: Ignore the "Footpath Sturminster Newton 2" sign and keep on a few more yards past Joyce's Coppice to the "Bridleway Wood Lane 3/4" sign where you turn right and go through the narrow wood and through the half-gate into the first field.   Take note of the "Keep to the Public Footpath" sign as the paths have recently been re-aligned.   Firstly, follow the edge of Joyce's Coppice, slightly uphill and through newly planted trees,   When the wide, grass track turns left uphill, keep straight on to find a half-gate with a Footpath arrow and a Bridleway arrow beyond it. This is the Public Footpath and you should now follow the LH, lower edge of this narrow field to the unmarked half-gate in the bottom RH corner.   Through this gate, follow the RH wood, row of trees and wire fence to the brow of the hill where there are views down to the River Stour and the short-cutters' route on your right.

1/4 mile after the brow, you will reach a Footpath-arrowed half-gate in the bottom RH corner, close to a small wood.   There may or may not be an electric fence which contains the path.   If there isn't, just keep close to the edges of this field as you pass around it.   Turn left alongside the small wood and walk up to join the Bridleway which runs from right to left up against the high-banked hedge.   Follow this RH hedge up to a farm gate and a Bridleway-arrowed half-gate in the hedge.   Go through the gate and keep to the LH hedge and bank, on top of which is a chain link fence bordering a barn yard.   There are good views towards Okeford Hill from here, just before you drop down to the gate in the far LH corner with a Bridleway arrow to "Cutt Mill 3/4" on the other side.   In the wide-verged gravel lane, turn left and walk uphill, passing cantilever gates and the concreted barn yard on your left as you go, past a Footpath-arrowed track coming from your right.

ROUTE 2: Turn sharp right to the "Footpath Sturminster Newton 2" stile and climb over onto the steep banked path which bears left between Joyce's Coppice and the cottage garden.   Look out for ditches if the grass and weeds (I mean wild flowers) are overgrown.   Now, begin a 2 mile stroll all the way back to Sturminster Newton where you will rejoin the starting path just after the part-demolished railway arches by Colber Bridge.   The Footpath is clearly marked at every stile on the way so, if you just keep close to the riverside and follow the arrows, I don't think I need to elucidate further - Just follow the Stage Maps.

40

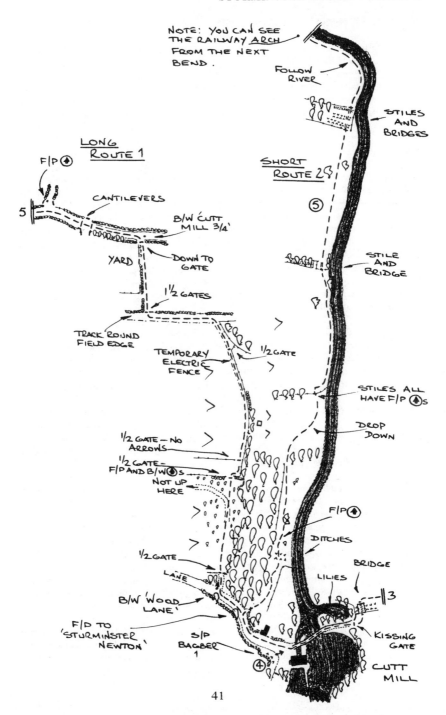

NOTE: YOU CAN SEE THE RAILWAY ARCH FROM THE NEXT BEND.

FOLLOW RIVER

STILES AND BRIDGES

LONG ROUTE 1

F/P

SHORT ROUTE 2

CANTILEVERS

B/W 'CUTT MILL 3/4'

DOWN TO GATE

YARD

STILE AND BRIDGE

1½ GATES

TRACK ROUND FIELD EDGE

TEMPORARY ELECTRIC FENCE

½ GATE

STILES ALL HAVE F/P s

DROP DOWN

½ GATE - NO ARROWS

½ GATE - F/P AND B/W s NOT UP HERE

F/P

DITCHES

BRIDGE

½ GATE

LILIES

LANE

B/W 'WOOD LANE'

F/D TO 'STURMINSTER NEWTON'

S/P BAGBER 1

KISSING GATE

CUTT MILL

41

STAGE 5

HINTON ST MARY TO HOME FARM

When you reach the B3092, cross carefully and join the LH elevated stone pavement up the hill into Hinton St Mary. At the top of the hill, there is a bench just past the "White Horse" so, sitting there or in the "White Horse", have a rest and a read. The village derives the first part of its name from a Saxon owner whilst the second part comes from the Abbey of St Mary in Shaftesbury which is recorded in the Domesday Book as holding *Haintone*. St Peter's church still has its 12thC font and a 15thC Perpendicular tower although it was extensively rebuilt by William Osborne in 1846.

The adjoining Manor House of 1695 is owned by the Pitt-Rivers family and was once home to the famed archaeologist George Pitt-Rivers but, long before him, it was owned by the mystical writer William Freke who specialised in the interpretation of dreams and produced a *Dictionary of Dreams*. Between 1683 and 1687, Freke fell foul of the legal and religious Establishments by publishing an eight-part essay which included "a clear and brief confutation of the Doctrine of the Trinity". He sent the essays to Members of Parliament who voted them to be burnt in the Palace Yard. Freke was bound over for 3 years and ordered to make recantation in the four Courts of Westminster Hall. He appears to have overcome this setback and, after his arrival in Hinton St Mary, he came to believe that he was a prophet. This doesn't seem to have induced any doubts about his worthiness, though, and he still became a Justice of the Peace for Hinton St Mary. He died in 1744 at the age of 82 and was buried in the churchyard next door to the Manor House.

Turning along the lane with thatched "Yeomans Wake" on the RH corner, follow the elevated path to St Peter's - it will probably be locked - and continue past the stone buttressed tithe barn to the high walled, ornate lodge gates with watchful bronze cranes or storks and the initials AH:PR for Pitt-Rivers. There is space for a few cars on the right as the beech avenue from the Manor House continues straight ahead to the B3092. Turn left onto the lane which is signposted "Manston 1.1/2" and follow the RH wooden fence and the staddle stone-edged lawn in front of the stone walls and summer house of the Manor on your left. Looking through the next ornate gates in the yew hedge, you will have a good view along the rows of pleached limes to the House. Hinton St Mary enjoys an elevated position and there is a superb panorama from here including Melbury Downs and Okeford Hill.

Follow the level lane along a line of ash trees on your left and, after a bungalow on your right, you enter the concrete surfaced yard of Manor Farm. A Footpath arrow near the large beech on your left points you straight along the yard track with numerous barns, silage and corn silos en route whilst, after the huge lime tree on your left, there are even better views to Duncliffe Hill, Shaftesbury and Melbury Beacon. Keep following the track until, after the last few barns, it becomes a slightly descending farm track with grass up the middle, confined between hedges at first, then with a wire fence on your right which allows long views towards Hambledon Hill and Okeford Hill A Footpath arrow on a gatepost by the LH opening confirms your direction as you descend to a gate with another Footpath arrow.

Halt awhile and look for the stile in the far, lower hedge, slightly right from your gate - or, for the technical , on a bearing of 110 degrees ESE. A path had been cut through the sweetcorn the last time I passed this way, so this bodes well for your success in crossing this field and finding the stile.

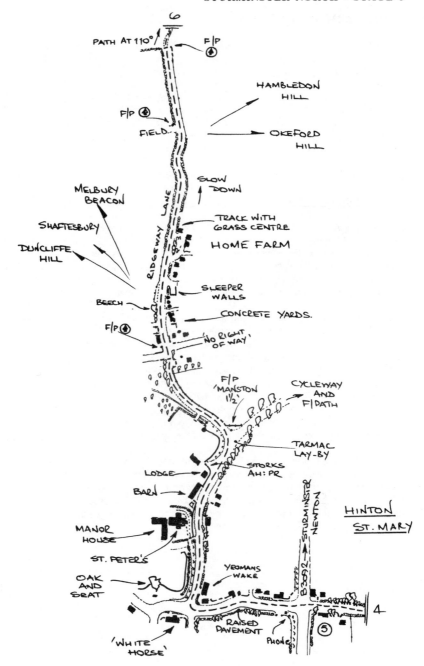

6

PATH AT 110°

F/P

HAMBLEDON HILL

F/P

OKEFORD HILL

FIELD

SLOW DOWN

MELBURY BEACON

TRACK WITH GRASS CENTRE

HOME FARM

SHAFTESBURY

DUNCLIFFE HILL

RIDGEWAY LANE

SLEEPER WALLS

BEECH

CONCRETE YARDS.

F/P

'NO RIGHT OF WAY'

F/P 'MANSTON 1½'

CYCLEWAY AND F/PATH

TARMAC LAY-BY

LODGE

STORKS AH: PR

BARN

HINTON ST. MARY

MANOR HOUSE

ST. PETER'S

STURMINSTER NEWTON

YEOMANS WAKE

B3092

OAK AND SEAT

'WHITE HORSE'

RAISED PAVEMENT

PHONE

⑤

4

43

STAGE 6

HOME FARM TO MANSTON

On arrival at the stile, follow the Footpath arrow straight on, not the white arrow to the right. Cross the field to the row of willows and hawthorns which flank Chivrick's Brook as it flows towards the River Stour. Go over the two, Footpath-arrowed stiles with the bridge between and cross the next, short field to the next unsigned stile in the facing wire fence. From here, look up the steep field to locate a farm gate in the top RH corner of the facing hedge and head straight up to it. If the field is planted, follow the edge anti-clockwise as this is the Footpath shown on the definitive map anyway. Half-way up, you will see the top of the lofty 15thC tower of St Gregory's church, Marnhull over to your left.

Go through the gate onto a wide, grassy track with a banked LH edge and a wire fence on the right. At the very top, a rough farm track turns sharp right and heads towards a distant gate whilst there is a tempting half-gate straight ahead down in the bottom LH corner of your field. Ignore them both! Instead, turn half right and peer into the distance towards the far end of this long field where you will see a very large oak tree in the far LH bottom corner. The Footpath runs through the farm gate which you will see about 25 yards to the right of this oak tree. Head for this gate and, when you get there, you'll see that it hasn't any arrows on or near it. This put me off on my first walk around here - especially as there was a huge brown bull with numerous wives on the other side - so I followed the track instead and got hopelessly lost.

So, go through or over the gate and aim for a spot about 100 yards along the high, deep LH hedge in this next field - you can't see it from here but there is a stile lurking in the hedge waiting for you. Go over the stile and fall down the drop into the ditch on the other side. Pick yourself up, climb over the stile facing you which brings you out into a descending field and stop again. Look down to the bottom RH corner of this field and head down there for a pair of iron gates which mask another stile (Footpath-arrowed this time). You may have noticed that these stiles have Footpath arrows on their other sides so you're OK if you're walking the other way. Anyway, follow the same line to a pair of stiles in a double wire fence - looking out for an inquisitive pony from the adjacent field with the open wooden fence.

Over these stiles, follow the same line again to an un-arrowed farm gate before some big oak trees in the adjacent right hedge. Go through the gate - or over, if it's tied up - and keep on the same line again, heading marginally left of the big oak tree up the hill. Just past the tree, bear around the left edge of a small clump of bushes wherein there is supposed to be a pond (according to the larger-scale maps) and you will see a gate in the corner of the joining hedges.

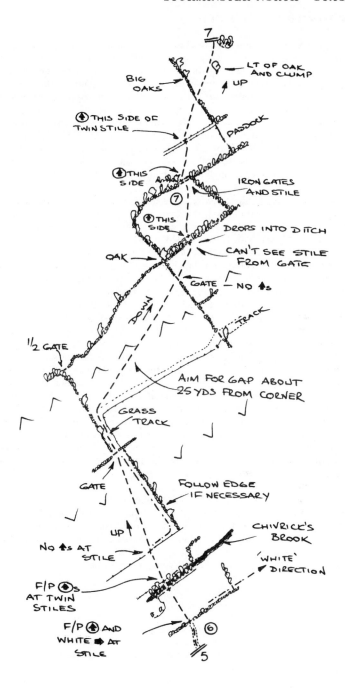

STAGE 7

MANSTON TO STOUR FIELDS

At the corner gate, look down the field towards your right and you will see a stile just after the third pair of houses.   Head straight for it and it will lead you into a narrow, fenced path between the garden of that last house and a detached house on your left. Squeezing past the electricity pole at the other end, drop carefully down into the busy B3091 Sturminster to Shaftesbury road, Manston - just opposite the Parish Notice board and a builder's yard.   Turn left and cross over the road, walking downhill towards the T-junction at the wood-fenced paddock on the RH corner where the B3091 turns sharply left.   At the "Manston" signpost, turn right (for "Child Okeford 2.1/2 and Blandford 9") and stroll for 250 yards along the level road, past the telephone box on your right and past several houses and the Old Rectory on your left, to a Footpath-arrowed track to your right, just before the bridge over Manston Brook.

The Brook and the River Stour border the grounds of Manston House and church, the entrance to both of which is just beyond the bridge, before the Footpath for "Hammoon and Child Okeford".   The ancient church is of Norman origin, mostly rebuilt in the 13thC and with a tower added in 1534.   The wagon roof of the aisle and nave dates back to the 15thC so there is much of interest to see here.   However, turn down the track with the cottage on the corner and with neatly tended trees and grass on your left in front of the Brook.   Follow the short track past turns into a RH bungalow and go through the facing, Footpath-arrowed gate next to the low stone barn.   Note "Dogs to be Kept on Lead" as you follow the grass track or the unclear path to the left of it across the first field, from both of which you can see the old church and parts of Manston House to your left.   The Footpath stile through the wire fence and the bridge across a ditch is near the Stour and you are supposed to keep close to the River for about 1/4 mile in this next field but, if the grass track is clear, you may prefer to follow it instead.   Clearly, the riverside path above the steep banks affords a more pleasant walk, with birds and bullrushes to see at the appropriate times, but you have to veer away from it about 200 yards before the end of this very long field, where the river last bends sharply away, and aim slightly right towards a single post with a yellow Footpath arrow on it - about 10 feet to the left of a thick hawthorn which is, in turn, about 50 yards left of the farm gate in the facing wire fence - for the technical again, on a 250 degrees WSW bearing from the last bend. You may find it altogether easier to follow the faint tractor track between these farm gates, veering slightly left when you see the Footpath arrow post.

You are now at the arrow post where a stile puts you onto a single-width concrete bridge across a wide ditch into the next field.   Cross the bridge and keep to the same direction (WSW) and you'll find a Footpath-arrowed stile in the deep hedge near the far RH end of this narrowing field.   Go over the stile, across the narrow bridge and over the stile on the other side (See Stage 8 for Stile X) into the field on the other side, immediately turning left back onto your original line.

SPECIAL NOTE:

If, and only if, a very large, obviously rejected and resentful bull stations himself between you and the Footpath post which marks the stile out of the long field, and closely watches your approach, follow the "Escape from Bull Only" line on the adjacent map.

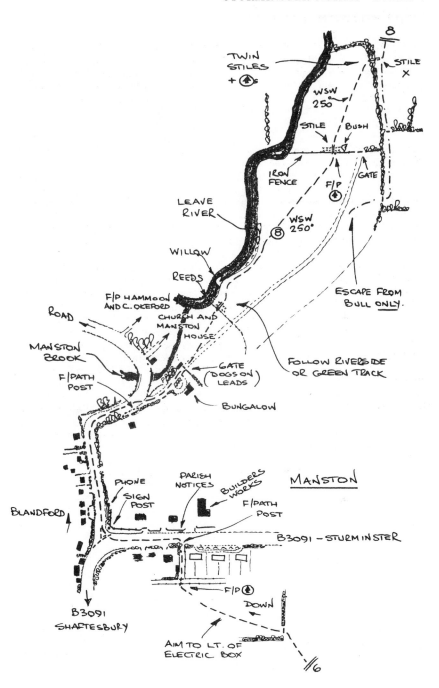

TWIN
STILES
+ ④s

8

STILE
X

WSW
250°

STILE   BUSH

IRON
FENCE

F/P
④

GATE

LEAVE
RIVER

WSW
250°
Ⓑ

WILLOW

REEDS

ESCAPE FROM
BULL ONLY.

ROAD

F/P HAMMOON
AND C. OKEFORD

CHURCH AND
MANSTON
HOUSE.

MANSTON
BROOK

GATE
(DOGS ON
LEADS)

FOLLOW RIVERSIDE
OR GREEN TRACK

F/PATH
POST

BUNGALOW

PHONE

SIGN
POST

PARISH
NOTICES

BUILDERS
WORKS

F/PATH
POST

MANSTON

BLANDFORD

B3091 - STURMINSTER

B3091
SHAFTESBURY

F/P ④

DOWN

AIM TO LT. OF
ELECTRIC BOX

//6

STAGE 8

STOUR FIELDS TO RIXON

At Stile X, look over the brow of the sloping field to your left and, between two long rows of bushes, you will see most of one big oak and the top of another. Big oak No.1 is nearer to you than big oak No.2 (see sketch) and you should aim for No.2, passing through much marsh grass on the way up and over the high field. You will see that No.2 lies in a banked hedge which runs away from you and you should walk along the RH side of this bank, at the far end of which you will find a Footpath-arrowed stile in the deep facing hedge.

Go over the stile, cross the long concrete footbridge and climb over the second stile halfway along it. From the end of the concrete strip, look straight ahead in exactly the same direction as you arrived (still 250 degrees WSW) and you will see, distantly I admit, a Footpath signpost over against the RH fence/hedge which comes in from your right. Walk towards this post through the long, level field. On the way, you'll cross a cattle path and you will arrive at the signpost which shows the way to "Sturminster Newton 1.1/2 and Manston Copse 1.1/2". Bear leftish along the hedge and follow it as it bends right towards a stile at the end of another high hedge.

Climb the arrowed stile and cross the brook to the second stile in the wire fence bordering the next field. That was Chivrick's Brook again. If you'd dropped a Poohstick into the brook earlier, it may have beaten you here. Anyway, head up the field towards the top LH corner where you will find a farm gate leading onto a steep, grassy track between a LH high beech hedge and a RH garden hedge. At the top, go over the stile and pass the Footpath sign for "Manston 1.1/2". You are now emerging back onto the B3091 with Sturminster Newton straight ahead. For your own safety, cross to the right and follow the pavement for just a few yards until, before the right turning road, you see a stile over on your left, signposted for "Railway Path 1/4".

Go over the stile onto the enclosed path between two gardens and follow it around a couple of right-angled bends. You then emerge onto a tarmac track which leads from Manston Road to farm buildings down on your left. Cross straight over the track into the descending, hedge-enclosed, grassy track opposite.

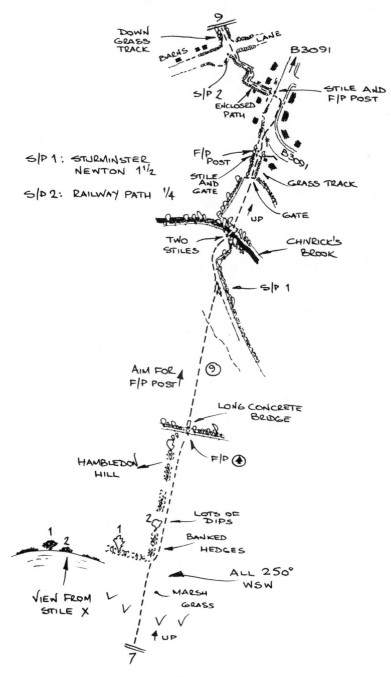

49

RIXON TO MARKET PLACE

On the way down this track, you pass between two wooden fence sections and past the gate of a fenced dressage and pony jumping arena on your left. Arriving at the bottom, climb over the Footpath-arrowed stile and bear right towards a gate which you will see past the end of the row of estate bungalows outside the field. You can see the tower of St Mary's, Sturminster Newton further off, between the gate and the end bungalow. When you go over the arrowed stile next to the farm gate, you will find yourself in a long field with the estate over the RH hedge. Aim for the single large willow ahead of you on the old railway embankment and, on the way, you will notice that the road (complete with pavements both sides) through the new estate suddenly stops at your field's RH fence. Clearly, the intention is to build on this field as well so, if you now face a housing estate, follow the diversions to the railway embankment underpass.

However, for now, still aiming for the willow, you will find a stile and wooden fence section next to a pair of Footpath arrows on a post before you reach the aforementioned tree. Go over this stile and walk under the railway arch, emerging on the other side at two more stiles, both with Footpath arrows. Take the right stile which leads into a small field with an electricity pole in the middle. Aim to pass this pole and you will arrive at another stile in the high hedge on the far side. If the field is planted and not cleared for you, go over the LH stile after the railway arch instead into the adjacent field, coming back into this field by the next right stile and following the edge of the field clockwise to this last stile of the day. The signpost points the ways for "Butts Pond (Industrial Estate) 1/4" and "Fiddleford Manor and Mill 1". Don't follow either, but go over the stile onto a narrow, hedge-enclosed tarmac path which will lead you, between houses and gardens to Penny Street and Gotts Corner. At the crossing, turn right into Penny Lane and continue up to Vine House on your right.

This long stone mullion-windowed cottage is where William Barnes was employed by the solicitor, Mr Dashwood, firstly to copy deeds in his admirable script. The Lane Fox Terrace row of cottages up on your left was once the Old Endowed School where Barnes was educated until 1814, when he left to join Mr Dashwood at the age of 13. At this point, you should bear sharp left for your visit to St Mary's although Penny Lane leads straight up to Market Place where you started your walk. Go past the gates to "Old School" (not Barnes' school) and "Dashwoods" and follow the path between the LH high stone walls and the RH clipped golden leylandii hedge. You then arrive at St Mary's. This is a larger church than those you have already visited which, although largely rebuilt in 1827, retained its 15thC nave and its North and South aisles. The tower base is also of the 15thC whilst the rest has been much restored. The old wagon roof of the nave displays admirable workmanship.

After your visit, continue along the footpath and past the inviting bench near the tower. Keep following the high brick and stone wall on your left but, when Church Lane goes straight ahead with a lovely thatched cottage with many colourful roses on the front on the RH corner, turn right. Walk past the long, stone Church Farmhouse on your right and the Wesleyan Chapel over on your left until you reach the open Pay and Display car park. Past here, you arrive at a T-junction with Penny Street which you left at Mr Dashwood's house. Turn left and follow the road round to Market Place where you started today's admirable journey. It has been a grand day out, hasn't it.

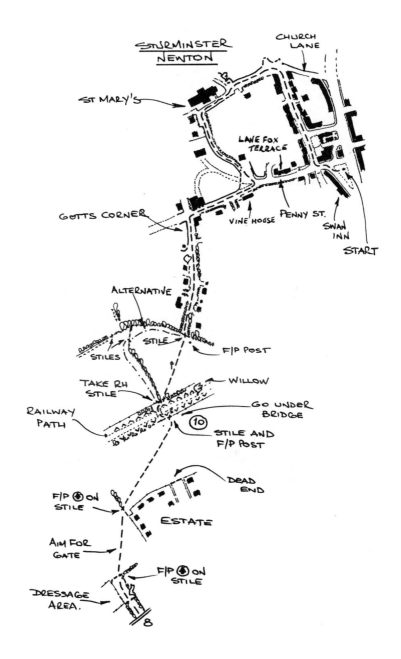

PART THREE - SOUTH OF SHERBORNE

INTRODUCTION

Having been much impressed on earlier visits to Sherborne by its beautiful Abbey, its pair of castles, the fine flower-filled gardens and the historic buildings which house the myriad private schools, I couldn't resist searching out some special walks which would revisit some of the fine viewpoints which I had found on *The Blackmore Vale Path*. Venturing further afield I have found some beautiful villages, farms, manor houses and churches which are all hidden "South of Sherborne". These include the village of Longburton strung along the Roman Road from Dorchester to Sherborne, 16thC West Hall, the hamlet of Folke with its little Ham stone church and a fine 15thC house and farm called "Font le Roi". The longer path also visits Kitford Bridge and Bishops Down on the way to Allweston, from where you call at Haydon Lodge before returning to Sherborne through Capability Brown's beautiful Deer Park.

THE ALTERNATIVES

Starting and finishing at the Tourist Information Centre in Digby Road - at Reference ST638164 on O S Map No. 183 - all three walks return through the superb Deer Park of Sir Walter Raleigh's beautiful Sherborne Castle II.

ROUTE 1: Total distance 11.1/4 miles. You leave Sherborne over the railway lines at the Station and head up Gainsborough Hill through Old Park Woods. Crossing Lovers' Grove and passing the North Wootton Lodge of the Deer Park, you then have an easy stroll down Green Lane Bridleway before crossing Caundle Brook for the first time and ambling through vast apple orchards on the way into Long Burton. Having visited the Parish Church of St James the Great, a parkland drive leads you past the fine 17thC West Hall en route to Folke. After Folke Manor House and St Lawrence's church, this Route extends the farmland stroll to cross Caundle Brook again, to visit Bishop's Down and to enjoy a leisurely walk along country lanes and along the old Caphay Drove. Crossing the A3030 at Marsh Court corner, there is a good view of the 15thC Font le Roi farmhouse and, after level fields and Blind Lane, the path joins up with Route 2 for the walk up Mundens Lane into Allweston. From there, an easy stroll brings you to Haydon where the ornate iron gates of Haydon Lodge open into the extensive deer park of the Digby estate for an easy, elegant return into Sherborne.

ROUTE 2: Total distance 8.3/4 miles. This Route differs from Route 1 by taking a shorter route from Folke Manor House to Mundens Lane and into Allweston - saving 2.1/2 miles on the way but missing out on a deep exploration of the Blackmore Vale.

ROUTE 3: Total distance 8 miles. Shortest of the walks, this misses the orchard walk into Long Burton, St James the Great's church and West Hall's park.

STAGE MILEAGES

STAGE	MILES	TOTAL MILES
ROUTE 1:		
1 Digby Road to Gainsborough Hill	.50	.50
2 Gainsborough Hill to North Wootton Lodge	1	1.50

STAGE MILEAGES (CONTINUED)

ROUTE 1 (CONTINUED)

3	North Wootton Lodge to Long Burton	1.25	2.75
4	Long Burton to Folke T	.75	3.50
5	Folke T to Caundle Brook	1.25	4.75
6	Caundle Brook to Caphay Drove	1	5.75
7	Caphay Drove to Font le Roi	1.25	7
8	Font le Roi to Allweston	.50	7.50
9	Allweston to Deer Park	1.75	9.25
10	Deer Park to Digby Road	2	11.25

ROUTE 2:

1 - 4	As Route 1 to Folke T	3.50	3.50
5	Folke T to Field Path	1	4.50
8	Field Path to Allweston	.50	5
9 - 10	As Route 1 Allweston to Digby Road	3.75	8.75

ROUTE 3:

1 - 2	As Route 1 to North Wootton Lodge	1.50	1.50
3	North Wootton Lodge to Green Lane End	1	2.50
5	Green Lane End to Folke T and Field Path	1.25	3.75
8	Field Path to Allweston	.50	4.25
9 - 10	As Route 2 Allweston to Digby Road	3.75	8

SOUTH OF SHERBORNE ROUTE LAYOUT

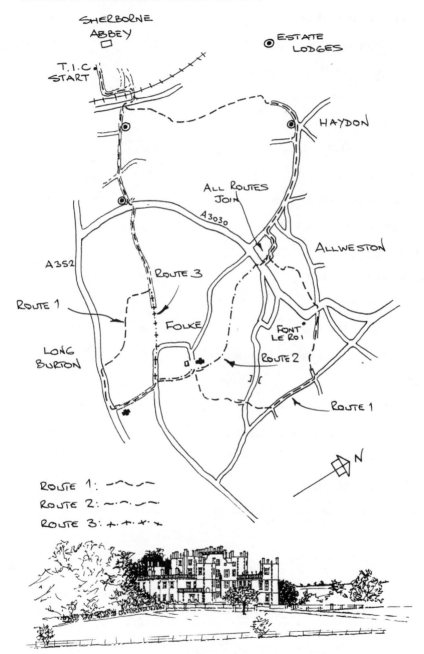

SHERBORNE
ABBEY

⊙ ESTATE
LODGES

T.I.C.
START

HAYDON

ALL ROUTES
JOIN

A3030

ALLWESTON

A352

ROUTE 3

ROUTE 1

FOLKE

LONG
BURTON

FONT
LE ROI

ROUTE 2

ROUTE 1

N

ROUTE 1: ⌒⌒⌒
ROUTE 2: ~⌒⌒
ROUTE 3: +·+·×·×

Sherborne "New' Castle

Parish Church of St James the Great, Long Burton

Abbey Church of St Mary the Virgin, Sherborne

55

STAGE 1

DIGBY ROAD TO GAINSBOROUGH HILL

Beginning outside the Tourist Information Centre in Digby Road, the Abbey Church of St Mary the Virgin is behind you.   Sherborne comes from *Scireburne* in the Domesday Book, from the Saxon for "clear stream".   Ina, king of the Saxons, founded a monastery here and "fixed an episcopal see" AD705.   This was later removed to Wilton, Old Sarum and, finally, Salisbury.   Bishop Roger de Caen appointed Thurstan to be Bishop of Sherborne and, at the same time, had the old church demolished, replacing it with a much larger, finer church of Norman design - the present, beautiful Abbey.   Much of Sherborne and district is owned by the Digby family whose family seat is in Minterne Magna in the South of Blackmore Vale and you will frequently come across their name as you wander around this area.

Now, walk down Digby Road, passing Digby Hall and the Day Centre over on your left.   Go past the conveniences and the garage on your right and past the Police Station and Magistrates Court on your left.   Then, either continue along Digby Road to Sherborne Railway Station at the end or divert through the iron gate into Pageant Gardens immediately after the Police Station.   Either way, follow the sign for "Riverside Walk to Old Castle 1/2" which stands outside the far gates of the Park. Cross over to the Station and follow the pavement round, past the platform gate and the telephone boxes, to go over the railway crossing by the signal box into Gas House Hill.   Keep to the RH pavement past "Hillside" and note the views on your left to the ruins of Sherborne Old Castle as you begin to go up the hill.   This Norman edifice was built on the site of the ancient palace of the Bishops of Sherborne by Roger, third Bishop of Salisbury, builder of the castle at Old Sarum and a favourite of Henry I.   Both buildings are actually more fortified palaces than military structures. After Roger fell from power, the Castle was held by the Crown for about 200 years but the Salisbury Bishops regained it in 1354.   At the dissolution of the monasteries, the property was forfeited so, by 1591, ownership of the castle had passed to Henry VIII's youngest daughter, Queen Elizabeth I, who granted it to Sir Walter Raleigh. He tried to modernise it but it was far too uncomfortable so he abandoned the project and began a conversion of an early Tudor hunting lodge which stood 1/4 mile South in the existing deer park.   This building became Sherborne "New" Castle which you will see on your return.   The Old Castle was besieged twice by Parliament during the Civil Wars and Cromwell later ordered its complete destruction.

Now, past the bench on the top RH corner, cross over the main road, signed "Dorchester A352 and Shaftesbury A30" and, next to the double Footpath-arrowed iron kissing gate, go between the twin barriers onto the wide tarmac path.   A sign advises that this is the way to "Terrace Playing Fields" as you begin a steady, uphill walk in an ever more wooded, ever steeper sided gulley with beech trees meeting overhead.   There are harts-tongue ferns in profusion in the upper slopes where the sides are 30 ft high and there is a Ham stone cliff face on your right.   Near the top, an iron fence appears on the LH slope and a RH half-gate leads into the hedged Terrace Playing Fields.   Following the main path, if you look across the Lodge garden by the electricity post, you will see the top of the New Castle.   Now, pass the Lodge gates and cross the tarmac drive which runs into Old Park Woods on the edge of the deer park.   Keep following a wide, grassy track alongside the iron Park Pale on your left, with a football ground now on your right, to an un-arrowed iron kissing gate which leads onto another long, grassy track with an open field on the right.

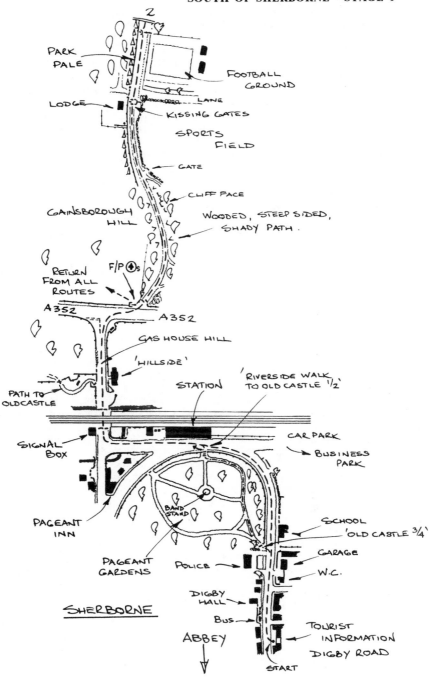

PARK PALE

FOOTBALL GROUND

LODGE

LANE

KISSING GATES

SPORTS FIELD

GATE

CLIFF FACE

GAINSBOROUGH HILL

WOODED, STEEP SIDED, SHADY PATH.

F/P ④s

RETURN FROM ALL ROUTES

A352

A352

GAS HOUSE HILL

'HILLSIDE'

PATH TO OLDCASTLE

STATION

'RIVERSIDE WALK TO OLD CASTLE ½'

SIGNAL BOX

CAR PARK

BUSINESS PARK

BAND STAND

PAGEANT INN

SCHOOL

'OLD CASTLE ¾'

PAGEANT GARDENS

POLICE

GARAGE

W.C.

SHERBORNE

DIGBY HALL

Bus

ABBEY

TOURIST INFORMATION

DIGBY ROAD

START

STAGE 2

GAINSBOROUGH HILL TO NORTH WOOTTON LODGE

On the other side of this field, there is another iron kissing gate which opens onto a neat, mown grass area which is maintained by the owner of the stone cottage with the garden and wooden sheds on your right.   Immediately and sharply left, there is the "Private" entrance onto the Park drive but keep straight on, up the increasingly steep, stony track through the banked edge of Old Park Woods.   About half-way up, there is a fine, thatched long-house on your right with two front doors where the wide, straight-through passage would have been.   Up on your left, a dry-stone wall runs parallel to the track before veering further away to the left as the banks become steeper and inhabited by harts-tongue ferns, especially along the ditch edges.

As you approach Lovers' Grove (the lovers in question remaining quite anonymous), you will be pleased to hear that you have completed the ascent out of Sherborne and that the track soon becomes level - and even downhill slightly.   The right turning at Lovers' Grove cross-tracks leads to West Hill toll-house on the corner of the A3030 Sturminster Newton Road and the A352 Dorchester Road.   I only mention this as an excuse to tell you about a rather unexpected series of searches which have been made over the years in this area - for coal.   Between the late 17thC and the late 18thC, four or five attempts were made to find coal at Pinford Hill and, 20 years after the latest failure on that site, a search was made at West Hill - also without success.

I have a pet theory about the West Hill site.   *South West of Shepton Mallett in Somerset, which is about 20 miles North of Sherborne and a major source of coal until recent years, there is a village called North Wootton.   One day, up walks the coalface master and says to the foreman, "Go and dig at North Wootton".   Now, the foreman is a Dorset lad and the only North Wootton that he knows is barely a mile from West Hill toll house.   So, off he goes and, of course, he doesn't find any.   Q.E.D.*

Now, cross over onto the wide, level grassy track and follow it, between low banks and high hedges.   There is a fine scots pine on your right on a gradual RH bend as the track begins a slight descent with views towards the Southern ridge of the Blackmore Vale, including Okeford Hill, Bulbarrow and the Dorsetshire Gap.   Further along the track, you reach the neat lawns and trimmed bushes of North Wootton Lodge.   Go through the iron kissing gate next to the high main gates and you will find yourself in the driveway entrance with a central lawn.   The A3030 runs towards West Hill on your right and a Footpath sign on the near left corner points to "Sherborne Station 1" and "Folke 1".   Turn left in the Folke direction and carefully cross over the road to the RH side where, just a few yards away, you will find a Bridleway-arrowed gate leading onto the wide, stony track which is Green Lane.

Follow the track, level to down-ish, between hedges and ditches with assorted odd trees in the RH hedge and with skylarks singing overhead.   The view towards the ridge is even better now and the radio aerials at 120 degrees East South East are definitely on top of Bulbarrow Hill.

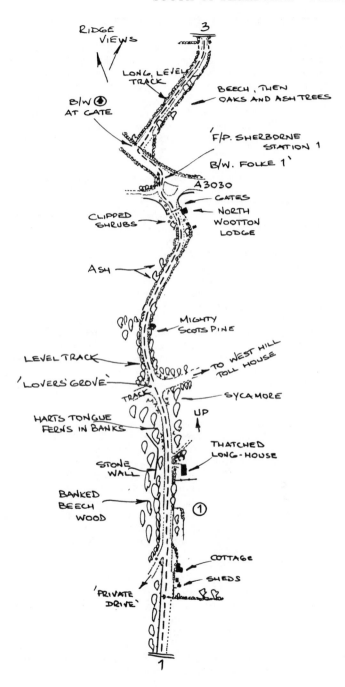

STAGE 3

NORTH WOOTTON LODGE TO LONG BURTON

Keep on going down the wide track with predominantly beech hedges, past a row of new beech trees and a small silage storage area on your left. You now arrive at Green Lane Coppice on your left and the track narrows and bends between the woods and a banked ditch on your right. After a few overhanging oak trees, the track widens again and you then reach an open area with a gap in the LH hedge and a gate in the RH hedge. Here is the first dividing of the ways. Routes 1 and 2 turn right past the triple Bridleway-arrowed post and through the gate into the RH field whilst the shortest Route 3 runs straight on down Green Lane. I'll take Route 3 first and then come back for Routes 1 and 2.

ROUTE 3: Keep on down until the track narrows and becomes a tree-lined, serpentine path, immediately crossing a strong wooden bridge over Caundle Brook. Just keep following the path for a comfortable 1/2 mile until you emerge onto a grass-filled 'spandrel' between right-angled hedges and the arc of a tarmac lane. Keep straight ahead and continue down the hedged lane.

ROUTES 1 AND 2: Through the RH gate, cross the field, slightly right of straight on, to the half-gate in the zig-zag wire fence opposite. Through the Bridleway-arrowed gate, you will see the reason for the saw-tooth line of the fence and the trees. A tributary of Caundle Brook meanders through these low fields and this is our first meeting with it today. Cross the brook by using the ford stones and go up the opposite bank to the half-gate. You now find yourself in the first of a great array of Long Burton apple orchards but, before you go on, remember the stones in the brook. Hutchins remarks that "there are some good stone quarries in the parish - much used for floors etc." Turn sharp left and keep close to the wire fence, ditch and high hedge which borders the orchard. Follow it round and join a gravel track, passing a pair of Bridleway arrow posts on a RH bend and walking up to a Bridleway-arrowed gate on the left where the track continues around the LH corner.

Go through the gate and follow the RH high hedge across an open field, past a single large oak, to another Bridleway-arrowed half-gate. Through the gate, another track comes up from the left and turns to lead you along the top RH hedge of another apple orchard with good views towards the wooded slopes of High Stoy and the hills around Buckland Newton. At the end of the orchard track, go through the last half-gate onto a short path which brings you out into Orchard Close, Long Burton. Keep straight on across the far corner of the Close and follow the road down between the older houses on the left and the newer houses (with a pavement) on the right. Past the LH electricity sub-station, the road narrows considerably between the LH hedge and the RH wooden garage so look out for cars in Quarry Lane - for such is the name of your road - as you approach the A352

You will notice that the sketch map does not purport to show houses, gates and driveway positions exactly. This is quite deliberate, mainly because it is the route which is important, not the positions of quite ordinary houses along it. (Notable houses are a different matter). Secondly, standing outside residential properties whilst making copious notes has led to some inquisitive, even antagonistic, approaches at times so I find it best all round if I keep walking whilst sketching suburban roads. That way, I'm less likely to be targetted by the local Home Watch members and you don't get assailed by too much detail.

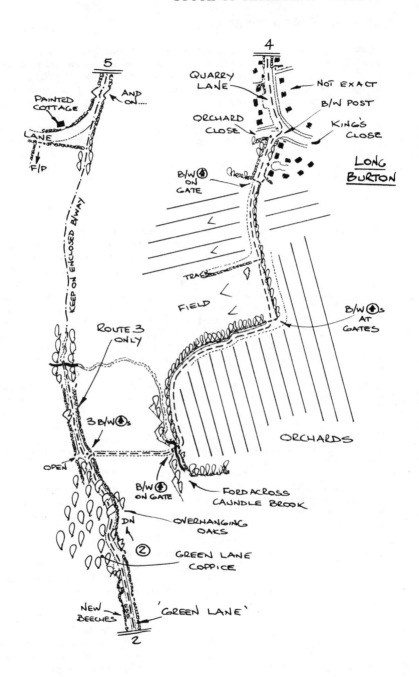

5

PAINTED
COTTAGE

AND
ON....

LANE

F/P

KEEP ON ENCLOSED B/WAY

ROUTE 3
ONLY

3 B/W④s

OPEN

B/W④
ON GATE

DN

②

NEW
BEECHES

'GREEN LANE'

2

4

QUARRY
LANE

NOT EXACT

B/W POST

ORCHARD
CLOSE

KING'S
CLOSE

LONG
BURTON

B/W④
ON
GATE

TRACK

FIELD

B/W④s
AT
GATES

ORCHARDS

FORD ACROSS
CAUNDLE BROOK

OVERHANGING
OAKS

GREEN LANE
COPPICE

STAGE 4

LONG BURTON TO FOLKE T

At the end of Quarry Lane, emerging opposite the "Dorset Works Organisation" yard, turn left onto the A352 and carefully walk along the un-pavemented roadway.   A little way down the road, a Footpath comes in from the stile in a LH field, just before the telephone box, and crosses the road to continue up Spring Lane opposite.   Now there is confirmation of that which you already knew - "No Footway for 200 yards".

Passing mostly stone cottages, some with thatched roofs, you arrive at the "Rose and Crown" standing on one side of the entrance to the West Hall estate whilst the "Long Burton Parish Church of St James the Great" stands on the farther side.   On the other side of the road, there is a bus shelter and an iron milestone which advises that it is 3 miles back to Sherborne.   Don't leave though as the best is yet to come.   If you would like to visit St James', the key is available from the keyholder nominated on the inside door in the porch.   Have a seat and I'll tell you about Long Burton.

The village stands in the ancient "Forest of the White Hart".   It doesn't appear in the Domesday Book and is believed to have been included in the See of Sarum at that time.   The church itself was "anciently a chapel of ease to Sherborne, dependent on it and dedicated to St James.   Before the Reformation, all the usual church rites were carried out here except burials - which took place at Sherborne."   The original church is of Norman origin although little remains.   The oldest part is the tower which has an Elizabethan or Jacobean top layer whilst a huge restoration of the rest of the fabric was completed in 1873.   There are two superb painted monuments in the chapel which was built by Leweston Fitzjames at the North of the chancel.   One is dedicated to his father Sir John who died in 1625 and his mother Joan.   The other is dedicated to his in-laws, the Winstons.   Leweston himself died in 1638.

Now, from the church, turn up the wide approach to the Lodge, high kissing gate and main gates which lead into the "Private Drive" of West Hall park.   Go through onto the tarmac drive for a lovely stroll through fine parkland.   Across the first open field, go through the gate in the chestnut-lined fence across the drive.   A row of fir trees stands on the other side of a dry-stone wall on your right.   Keep straight on down and up the other side of a shallow valley with the dry-stone wall on your right and open parkland on your left.

Beyond the stone wall, you will have intermittent views of 17thC West Hall.   Sadly, and I quote Nicholas Pevsner "Restoration and additions of 1924 seriously damage the house's visual effect".   Prior to that, the house was owned by several notable families whilst the manor of West Hall (and an earlier property) was owned by Henry Moleyns at his death as far back as November 1595.   After that, the present property was "the principal seat of the Mullins (*Moleyns*) of ancient descent in these parts": Coker.   Later, it was sold in 1741 to "Rev John King, formerly of Glanvilles Wootton, who repaired the mansion house which passed to his son Rev Henry King": Hutchins.   The entrance doorway is marked with deep chops made by Roundheads on a visit in 1645 - according to family tradition.

Right then - keep on up the drive, past the gated entrance to the house, and now with an iron estate fence on your left.   At the top of the hill, you arrive at a converted barn and, through the gate with a pond and wooden fence on its right, continue past dairy buildings on the left and a ramp for loading 'effluent launching vehicles'.

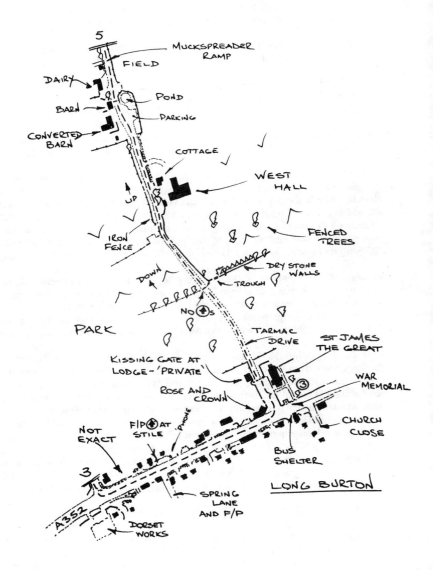

5

MUCKSPREADER RAMP

FIELD

DAIRY

BARN

CONVERTED BARN

POND

PARKING

COTTAGE

UP

WEST HALL

IRON FENCE

FENCED TREES

DRY STONE WALLS

DOWN

TROUGH

NO ®s

PARK

TARMAC DRIVE

ST JAMES THE GREAT

KISSING GATE AT LODGE - 'PRIVATE'

WAR MEMORIAL

ROSE AND CROWN

③

NOT EXACT

F/P ® AT STILE

PHONE

CHURCH CLOSE

BUS SHELTER

3

LONG BURTON

A352

SPRING LANE AND F/P

DORSET WORKS

STAGE 5

FOLKE T TO CAUNDLE BROOK OR FIELD PATH

ROUTES 1 AND 2: With a ruined stone barn on the LH corner, you arrive at a T-junction with the Folke to Bishop's Down lane crossing from left to right.   So, turn left and, almost immediately, turn off the road at the Footpath arrow and go up the steps in the steep right bank.   Now, read on - from "Everybody"......

ROUTE 3: Before the T-junction to West Hall, turn left up the signed steps in the bank and decide on Route 1 or 2 when you get to the church.   Now. read straight on...

EVERYBODY: At the top, follow the LH edge of the field, along the hedge with gaps in it.   You then arrive at a wooden gate (with no Footpath arrows) which leads into a long, wide field.   Keep straight on, along the LH hedge, wooden fence and following stone walls, past the long stone cottage and barn combination and past the lovely garden of Folke Manor House - all on your left.   All the way, there are fine views on your right to the South and East ridges which border the Blackmore Vale.

Arriving at the gate and kissing gate, go through onto the wide grassy area which becomes an avenued tarmac path leading up to the Manor House and St Lawrence's church.   The house is private but you can visit the church if you collect the key from the address advised outside.   There was a chapel on this spot in 1291 and Dean Chandler's Register of 1405 records its consecration in honour of St Lawrence.   The present church was built in 1628 of fine golden Ham stone and, although restored in 1875, it retains some original Charles I period fittings - and an air of tranquility.

Returning to the signpost by the kissing gate, you now have to decide whether you want to walk directly to Allweston or enjoy a meander over some enchanting farmland, twice crossing Caundle Brook and following a wide drove road on the way - it's only 2.1/2 miles more and I enjoyed every step.   So, completely unbiased, I'll take Route 1 ramblers first whilst Routes 2 and 3 continue at the bottom of the page.

ROUTE 1: Go through the kissing gate and look across the descending field, with the fenced wood on your left, to find a wooden stile in the hedge - 280 yards away.   Go over the unmarked stile, over the ditch and over the second stile and stop.   Now aim for the RH end of the thick group of large trees down the hill.   Look out for the ditch which runs down from over on your left to join the end of these trees.   You want to meet at almost the same spot - on bearing 140 degrees South East.   Then follow the ditch as a facing high hedge steers you leftwards.   With the field narrowing, you will see a 1/2 gate facing you and another leading you into the hedge.   Go through the hedge gate and cross the wooden bridge which spans Caundle Brook - on its way to join the River Lydden which is en route to join the River Stour and, ultimately, the English Channel.   On the other side of the bridge, bear left into a wild meadow field.

ROUTES 2 AND 3: Don't go through the kissing gate.   Turn left through the farm gate and follow the LH wall and wooden fence to the corner stile with a sleeper across the ditch.   Now follow the wire fence to a Footpath-arrowed stile onto a crossing farm track.   Cross over the track and follow the field path on the RH side of the long stone wall, North at first then bending left to the East.   A pair of stiles and a substantial wooden bridge span a wide ditch in the deep hedge facing you and you now keep to the LH edge of the field, bending further left to a Footpath-arrowed stile and bridge across another hedged ditch and bank.   From here, keep to the LH edge of this next field.

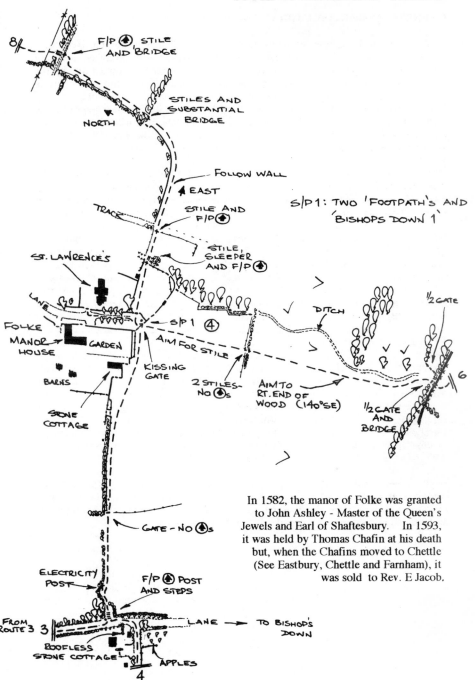

In 1582, the manor of Folke was granted to John Ashley - Master of the Queen's Jewels and Earl of Shaftesbury.   In 1593, it was held by Thomas Chafin at his death but, when the Chafins moved to Chettle (See Eastbury, Chettle and Farnham), it was sold to Rev. E Jacob.

65

STAGE 6

CAUNDLE BROOK TO CAPHAY DROVE

Walk through this narrow, probably high-thistled and marsh-grassed, field with Caundle Brook on your left and a high hedge on your right. Not far away, there is a field gate on your right which leads into an uphill field but keep on a little further until you see a stile near the deep, tree-packed RH corner. Past this stile, there is another immediately afterwards. Go over it into a long, wide, steep field (There's a Footpath arrow on the other side so you're on the right path) and bear right towards the top corner of the field. When you reach the farm gate, you will find a Footpath arrow and a Bridleway arrow on the other side. Go through the gate onto a hedged, grassy track which leads to the tarmac Down Lane.

Down the lane to your left, Caundle Brook flows under Kitford Bridge on its way to meet you again at Pin Bridge. Don't go down the lane though, but cross over Down Lane to the LH of the two gates facing you - or, if you'd rather, you can turn right and walk up the lane to the next T-junction (where the road comes from the earlier West Hall T-junction) and turn left onto the Bishop's Down lane. However, we're going through the LH gate into the field with a hedge on the RH side - running South East. There is another gate near the oak tree in the far RH corner. Go through this gate and bear slightly left across the next field, on an almost due East bearing and ignoring the first gate over on your right (or walking around the edge of this field anti-clockwise if you prefer) to a farm gate which brings you out onto a very wide, specimen tree-planted verge on the lane at Bishop's Down. Turn left onto the lane just before a right-turning lane runs off to "Ryall's Farm". Enjoy a gentle, slightly downward stroll along the main lane, past "Pheasants Cottage" on your left and past a Footpath-arrowed stile in the RH hedge.

The verges are extremely wide as you approach a right bend in the road and a hedge-enclosed track runs down to a gate on the left. After the bend, there is a group of willows in a dip on the RH side and, after the two gates on your right, a very large oak stands in a deeper dip on the near RH corner of a staggered crossing. You need the LH turning which is Caphay Drove whilst the next turning right leads up to "Bensham Farm". In various guises, (mostly very wide due to the meandering cattle or driven sheep) Caphay Drove runs for 1 mile straight to the junction of tracks and roads from Font le Roi Farm, Marsh Court and Allweston.

Begin your journey along Caphay Drove on a descending tarmac surface between banked hedges with just a RH verge at first. After a LH gate, there are large oaks in the verges on both sides and you will notice that there are huge oaks scattered all about in the hedges and singly, park-like, in the fields as well.

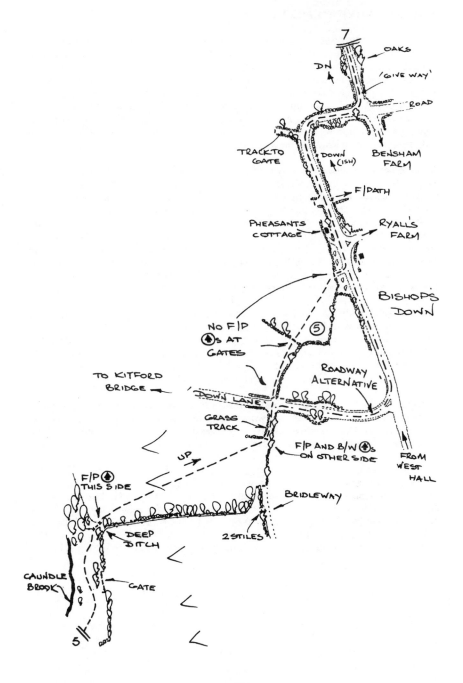

STAGE 7

CAPHAY DROVE TO FONT LE ROI

Keep on down the wide, verged lane until the tarmac runs out at the solitary farm cottage on your left. Then continue down on the wide, grassy track between distant hedges (is that a passing place for coaches or cattle on the left before the RH gate?). There are now ditches on both sides as the Drove widens on the approach to Pin Bridge with a willow tree on its left. Cross the stone slab (which is Pin Bridge) over Caundle Brook again and you are on a narrow, winding path through a small wood with a somewhat boggy area about halfway through. However, you are soon out again, joining a narrow, hedged-in section of Caphay Drove with some overhanging oak trees and with a low field on your left.

You soon emerge onto a wider area with old, painted stone Caphays Cottage down on your left, just before the altogether tidier "Caphays House' and its adjoining converted barn. Keep straight on, now a verged tarmac lane with a row of oaks on the right and a solitary ash on the left. Before a bend in the lane, the hedges distance themselves from you even further and stay that way until you reach a crossing of the A3030 Sherborne to Sturminster road with the tree-edged driveway to Marsh Court on the opposite RH corner. If you look along the A3030 to your left, you will see the lovely, originally 15thC, Font le Roi house but, being surrounded by barns, you have a better view of it as you cross the next field. This used to be Fauntleroy's Marsh but, when you cross the road, you will see you are now on the verge of Caundle Marsh.

The available family tree of the Fauntleroys begins at John who died in 1440 (from the Visitation Book of Elizabeth I's time). However, the family is said to descend from King John of France who was imprisoned in Jersey in 1357 by Edward III following his capture in battle at Poitiers during the 100 years war with France. The Queen of France was delivered of a son in Jersey whilst negotiating John's release. Derivation of the name Fauntleroy: Font le Roi = l'enfant du roi = child of the king.

Nicholas Pevsner was very impressed with Font le Roi because its rubble-stone fabric is "unrestored, so that one can see what beauty of texture Folke's other two houses have lost (Folke Manor and West Hall)". Several sections of the 15thC and 17thC still remain, including the 15thC gateway.

For now, though, concentrate on crossing the main road to the security of the verge on the opposite LH corner where you will find the sign for "Caundle Marsh" and all that remains of a DCC signpost - the location number 674137. Go through the un-arrowed gate next to the "Caundle Marsh" sign and look for a far distant gate in the opposite hedge (at 320 degrees North West - or left of straight on) about 300 yards away. Reaching this gate, go through and keep to the same direction for another 250 yards to the far corner where you will find a deep ditch before - and in - the hedge.

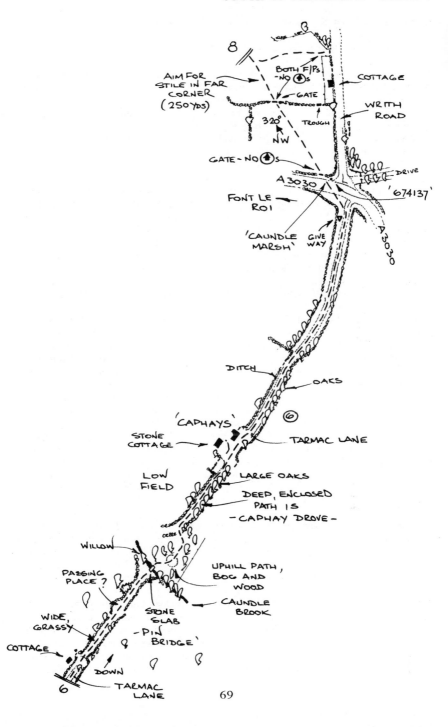

8

AIM FOR
STILE IN FAR
CORNER
(250 YDS)

BOTH F/Ps
-NO ⊙s

COTTAGE

GATE

WRITH
ROAD

320°

NW

TROUGH

GATE - NO ⊙s

A3030

'674137'

DRIVE

FONT LE
ROI

'CAUNDLE
MARSH'

GIVE
WAY

A3030

DITCH

OAKS

'CAPHAYS'

STONE
COTTAGE

⑥

TARMAC LANE

LOW
FIELD

LARGE OAKS

DEEP, ENCLOSED
PATH IS
- CAPHAY DROVE -

WILLOW

PASSING
PLACE ?

UPHILL PATH,
BOG AND
WOOD

CAUNDLE
BROOK

WIDE,
GRASSY

STONE
SLAB
- PIN
BRIDGE'

COTTAGE

DOWN

TARMAC
LANE

6

69

STAGE 8

FONT LE ROI OR FIELD PATH TO ALLWESTON

Be certain of which Route you are following - then read on:

ROUTE 1: There is a stile in the hedge - so look carefully and then scramble down the ditch and over the stile on the high bank. There are no Footpath arrows yet but there will be some later to relieve any concerns you may have. So, out into the next field, look across and aim to the left of the high wire fenced enclosure over the opposite hedge. In about 250 yards, you will reach a pair of stiles which lead you out onto a lane which is gravel to the left and grassy up on your right, after the wire-fenced enclosure opposite. In the lane, you will see that there is a Footpath arrow on the stile that you have just left - I told you.

Cross the lane to the hedge, to the left of the enclosure entrance, and go through a gap (no stile, no gate, no arrows) and keep to the RH hedge and ditch as you follow this longish, uppish field to the top RH corner where there is a working yard over the other side and rows of houses and gardens facing you. Follow the edge of the field round to the left, as instructed by the Footpath arrows in the corner, and you soon arrive at a banked opening up to an enclosed - and signed - Footpath before a wood-fenced paddock. Go up into the path, between the paddock and a leylandii hedge, and follow it to its end, passing a low stone barn on your left, where you descend on a stone step with a Footpath arrow post into Mundens Lane, Allweston. Turn right.

ROUTE 2: You will find another Footpath-arrowed stile in the banked hedge in the LH corner and, when you are over it, bear right and follow a path slightly to the right of the line of electricity wires towards the top, nearest of two, RH corners - aiming at first somewhere left of the 3-windowed, two-gabled stone cottage - near the far hedge. Due North East, if you have a compass. If the field is planted, you may find it easier (as normal in these conditions) to go anti-clockwise around the edge. In any event, you will eventually arrive at a gateway in the banked hedge in the top RH corner. Go through the gate and continue in the same (North East) direction - or around the LH edge - until you arrive about 20 yards to the left of the top RH corner. Here you will find probably the most dangerous stile in existence. It's not that it isn't strong enough or anything like that. It's that the A3030 is down the steep bank on the other side and you'll have to decide when it's safe to cross the road in the same instance as you decide to drop down into the road. I should think that the sight of a rambler perched high up in the hedge as his/her vehicle sweeps around the bend in the road must give the most experienced driver palpitations as well.

So, thinking, dropping, dashing across and heaving a sigh of relief (all at once), turn right on the opposite verge and head down to the first left turning with the banked tree on the corner and the stone cottage - which turns out to be a bakery - beyond it. Turn left onto "Mundens Lane" and walk up the hedge-bordered lane, past a yard of stone barns and a signed Footpath descending from a hedged alley on your right.

ROUTES 1 AND 2: All together now, follow Mundens Lane down and up, left, right and left again, passing several very pretty gardens and long dry stone walls on the way. At the large area of garages on the last LH bend, where a signed Footpath goes straight on, keep following the road up past more cottages to join the Allweston to Haydon road as it crosses your path with Vincents Close on the opposite side. Turn right and be ready for some inquisitive looks from the residents of Allweston.

70

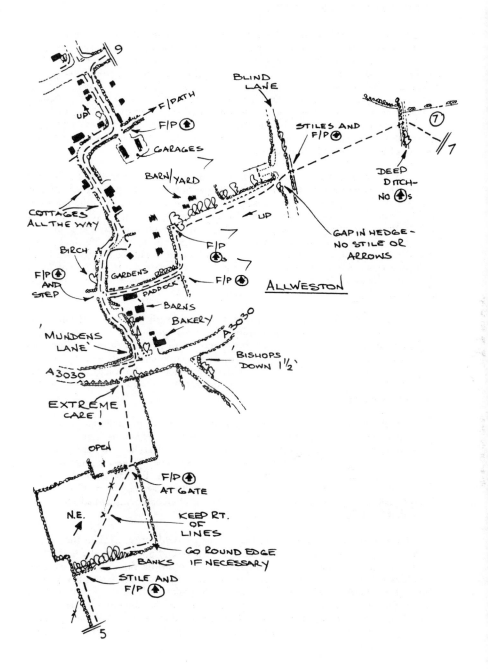

STAGE 9

ALLWESTON TO DEER PARK

Keep to the main road through Allweston whilst noticing that the Stage Map is not an exact representation of every house or gate as you pass through. However, I'm sure a short break sitting on the bench under the tree in Roselyn Crescent will be O K. whilst you read about Allweston. Alveston (Allweston) derives from *Eanulfeston*, meaning Eanwulph's town, from the name of a Saxon lord. In 1391, Nicholas Fauntleroy held half a virgate of land here (a virgate being about 30 acres). Passing down through the Fauntleroys, the land was eventually devised to Mr George Cooper of Sherborne who sold it, with Fauntleroy's Marsh Farm, to the trustees of Thomas, Viscount Weymouth. Thence it went to the Marquis of Bath and finally to the Digbys of Sherborne and Minterne Magna.

Now, on the road again, carry on out of Allweston along the hedged and un-verged road. The signpost at the "Wenlock" road intersection could keep you busy all day. It's packed with information but you need to follow the main route, bending leftwards for "Haydon 3/4". Past the stone cottage and the low stone barn on your right after it, keep on up the high-hedged road with a narrow verge on your left and a ditch on your right, passing various gates and alternating verges on the way. The hedges are still mainly beech and elderberry as you pass a bungalow and then a wooden fence with good views into low parkland on your right. A sign on the RH bank proclaims "Haydon - Caution Children and Animals" but it doesn't say which are the most dangerous.

Progressing along the road, there is a fine, long stone barn with red brick dressings on the roadside to your right followed by typical village houses to right and left. Further along, there is another pair of iron-fenced, twin-gabled houses on your right where a pavement begins, followed by a long stone, castellated wall with pillars and heavy wooden gates leading into the hidden grounds of the Victorian Rectory. Opposite these gates, there is a turning off to the left after a brick corner house with a telephone standing outside.

Keep straight on and you will see the now defunct chapel of St Katherine which has, apparently, recently been leased out by Lord Digby. Hutchins writes that "St Katherine's is a small ancient building in the early English style. In the churchyard there is the base and broken shaft of an ancient cross" - but this present building only dates from 1883, over 100 years after Hutchins. Thomas French, vicar of Haydon, was buried here on 2nd April 1635 whilst the church register begins in 1707 around the time that the Digbys first became patrons of the church, having gained the manor of Haydon from Thomas Chafe in the late 17thC.

After the fine scots pine in the iron-fenced chapel field, cross over to the verged Haydon Lodge entrance to Sherborne Castle deer park and go through the high black iron kissing gate onto the "Private" tarmac drive. Follow the drive straight on, past a World War II brick building and an ancient oak with a massive girth on your left. This high level driveway has fine views across the park to valleys and woods on your right as you continue to where the drive bears round in that direction. Here, keep straight on, away from the main drive - which is marked "Private" - past the Footpath arrows on your immediate left and into the beginnings of a wood with pine trees to the left of your track.

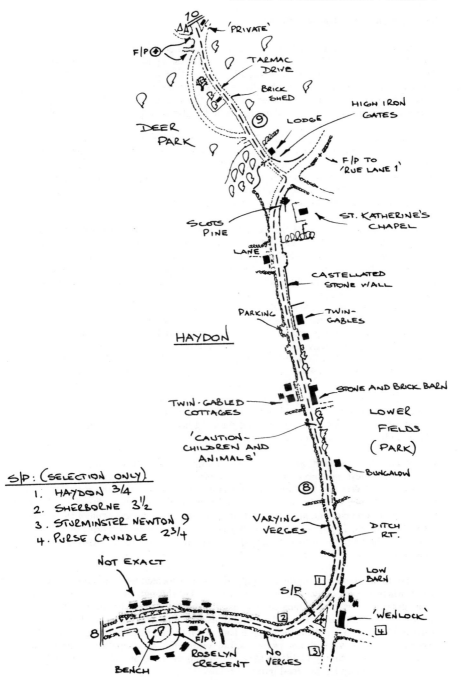

STAGE 10

DEER PARK TO DIGBY ROAD

Ignore all of the turnings off from the main route and continue past the weighbridge, the office and the wide clearing with the collection of high corrugated iron and asbestos buildings.   Follow the Footpath-arrowed tarmac and concrete path beyond this area into the mixed pine and deciduous wood with many concrete bases and tracks in the undergrowth.   There was an American Military hospital within these woods during the Second World War and a large camp for displaced persons - mainly Polish.

After a while, a wider track turns off to your left alongside a wire fence.   Keep straight on though, along an earthier path along the LH wire fence at first but then winding through the woods with a brick-built water tower over on your left.   Around the bends and past another shed on your right, you arrive at a pair of gates and another high kissing gate.   Out of the woods, you are on Jerusalem Hill from where there are fine views over the Blackmore Vale lowlands towards Yeovil.

Now, still on the track, cross the open field to a steep, bracken-covered slope with grassy tracks turning off to right and left.   Down the hill, you will see the old, iron-fenced, thatched hunting lodge on your left.   Hunting was strictly by special invitation of the Digbys but, with the fallow deer population down to 280 during the patronage of F J B Wingfield-Digby in the 1860s, the days of hunting parties were slowly drawing to a close.   Go through the high wooden kissing gate and keep straight on down, alongside the high deer fence and with a vast oak up on the left slopes before you reach the narrow end of a large fenced wood.   Go through the next high, wooden kissing gate and leave the tarmac driveway behind.   You are now on a LH wire fenced gravel track which descends continuously to Sherborne "New" Castle which you can see down on your right, next to its huge lake in the beautiful Park which was built by Capability Brown between 1756 and 1790.   Steadily descending, go through another kissing gate and just keep going until, on a right bend with a "Private" track going left through a fenced gate and another gate into the field ahead, bear right around the small wood and turn instantly left through the kissing gate into the low field with a bare oak over on your right.   I hope you took the opportunity to take a photograph of the New Castle.

As I mentioned at the start, Sir Walter Raleigh converted an old hunting lodge which stood on a limestone knoll into a comfortable castle.   Unfortunately, he was imprisoned in 1603 and his home was forfeited to King James I who gave it to his son, Henry, Prince of Wales but he died two years later.   It then passed to Robert Carr, Earl of Somerset but, after his fall from grace in 1617, James granted the whole estate to Sir John Digby at a knock-down price - but then the King did owe Digby money.   The Digbys added the four wings and the low hexagonal towers at their outermost corners which you now see.

Now, go up the steep field to the kissing gate which is located near the end of the top wood, where the iron fence gives way to wire.   Go through the gate and join the clear, grass path as it descends almost parallel with the road to the Castle gates. (Don't go straight down the hill to the steps intended for those heading for the Milborne Port road)   Follow the sloping path down to find the kissing gate with the two Footpath arrows which you passed before joining the tarmac path up through the canyon to Terrace Playing Fields on Stage 1.   From there, return across the road and railway lines and up Digby Road into Sherborne.

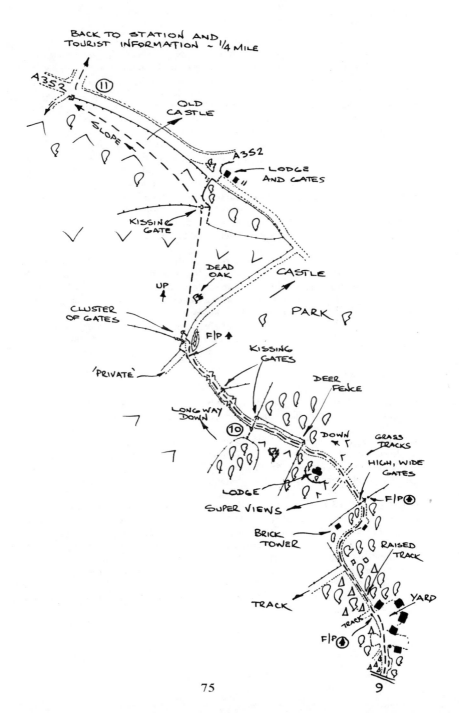

BACK TO STATION AND
TOURIST INFORMATION ~ 1/4 MILE

A352

(11)

OLD
CASTLE

SLOPE

A352

LODGE
AND GATES

KISSING
GATE

DEAD
OAK

CASTLE

UP

CLUSTER
OF GATES

PARK

F|P

'PRIVATE'

KISSING
GATES

DEER
FENCE

LONG WAY
DOWN

(10)

DOWN

GRASS
TRACKS

HIGH, WIDE
GATES

F|P

LODGE

SUPER VIEWS

BRICK
TOWER

RAISED
TRACK

TRACK

YARD

TRACK

F|P

9

PART FOUR - EASTBURY, CHETTLE & FARNHAM

INTRODUCTION

This pair of walks is the result of an urge to go back to a part of *The Cranborne Chase Path* which I had really enjoyed and wanted to explore further.   Being a long-distance path, there hadn't been the opportunity to wander far from the straight and narrow but these two circular walks lead you over what Ralph Wightman calls "The Dry Uplands" which stand above the Tarrant Valley and include the small villages of Chettle and Farnham.   These two villages have resisted expansion even though the forests which enclosed them during the hey-day of Cranborne Chase's deer hunts have been heavily forested over the years and are now much less dense.   This is still deer country though and single beasts or small groups will probably be found grazing the field and wood margins - if you go quietly.   This is high country and there are constant long-distance views over surrounding countryside and woodland.   Up here, you are accompanied by buzzards, skylarks and ever-argumentative rooks whilst, on occasions, you may hear woodpeckers and yellow hammers.   There are visits to three lovely churches and to see the remains of Eastbury House and the fine Queen Anne Chettle House as well as Bronze-Age barrows and the site of a bloody battle between 18thC Chase keepers and a group of determined poachers.

Now, how do you get to the starting point at the Tarrant Gunville T-junction (at Reference ST926127 on OS Map No. 195)?   If you go by car, there are a few spaces at St Mary's church entrance but leave room for worshippers and staff.   Alternatively, park carefully and with consideration along the edge of the valley road after the T-junction.   You could catch Wilts and Dorset Bus Nos. 182,184 and 185 to Tarrant Hinton and walk to the start or use Local Bus Nos. 323 and 403 which will take you directly to Tarrant Gunville.   Another option, for the Route 1 extension, would be to get off the 323 in Chettle, start there and walk back to Tarrant Gunville.

THE ALTERNATIVES

Beginning at Tarrant Gunville and following paths and tracks through the Eastbury estate to Chettle House, the Routes then divide for the long or short alternatives:

ROUTE 1: Total distance 5.3/4 miles.   This Route uses grassy Footpaths and Bridleways past Vanbrugh's Eastbury House and around Chettle Long Barrow en route to Chettle House before returning, across high fields and down chalky farm tracks, to the easy, level road past the reputedly haunted entrance gates to Eastbury House.

ROUTE 2: Total distance 9.1/2 miles.   This Route turns off at Chettle House to visit St Mary's Church and then wanders along pleasant Footpaths and Bridleways to the old Pitt-River's Museum at Farnham, where the little church of St Laurence also beckons.   A fine, high walk with wonderful views then takes you through a historic settlement, past an ancient oak forest and along easy tracks to the aptly named and deeply evocative Bloody Shard Gate.   After more high tracks across quiet farmland (apart from the skylarks), the Route descends back to Tarrant Gunville on a superb, soft and grassy track.   A short wander through the village then brings you back to the start for a welcome visit to St Mary's, Tarrant Gunville.

STAGE MILEAGES

STAGE	MILES	TOTAL MILES
ROUTE 1:		
1 Tarrant Gunville to Little Wood	1.25	1.25
2 Little Wood To Chettle and Eastbury Farm	2.75	4
3 Eastbury Farm to Tarrant Gunville	1.75	5.75
ROUTE 2:		
1 - 2 As Route 1 to Chettle	2.50	2.50
4 Chettle to Pitt-Rivers Museum	1.50	4
5 Pitt-Rivers Museum to Farnham	1.25	5.25
6 Farnham to Hatt's Coppice	1.75	7
7 Hatt's Coppice to Marlborough Lane	1.75	8.75
8 Marlborough Lane to Tarrant Gunville	.75	9.50

Chettle House (from Route 1 path)

77

EASTBURY, CHETTLE AND FARNHAM ROUTE LAYOUT

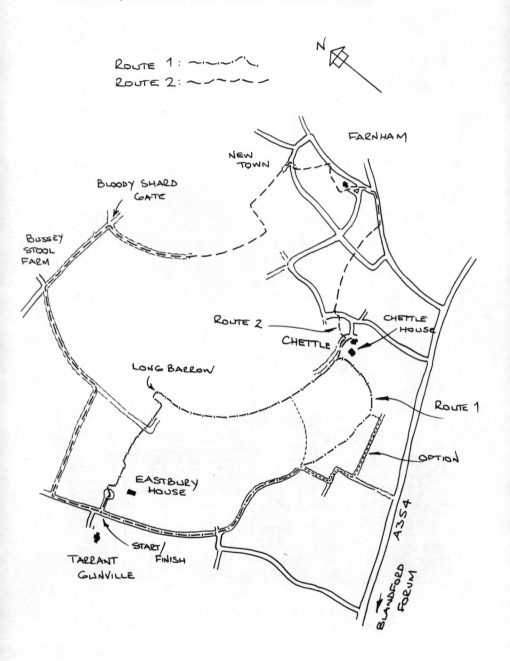

ROUTE 1: ~·~·~·~·
ROUTE 2: ~~~~~~

N

FARNHAM

NEW TOWN

BLOODY SHARD GATE

BUSSEY STOOL FARM

ROUTE 2

CHETTLE HOUSE

CHETTLE

LONG BARROW

ROUTE 1

OPTION

EASTBURY HOUSE

A354

START/ FINISH

TARRANT GUNVILLE

BLANDFORD FORUM

St Mary's Church, Chettle

Gateway to Eastbury House

STAGE 1

TARRANT GUNVILLE TO LITTLE WOOD

Starting at the signposted T-junction below St Mary's church, turn down the road with the infant River Tarrant in the LH ditch and turn left at the Footpath signpost into School Lane. The railings on the right border Eastbury Park but I'll tell you more about that in a few minutes. Walk up the hill, past cottages and a LH Footpath just before the Old School on your left. At the top, you reach School Close. Turn up the drive at the first of many Jubilee Trail arrows to the right of No. 7 and, at the garages, go past the "Footpath to Chettle" sign by a farm gate and a half-gate, to follow the track between the LH field and the backs of the School Close houses. Bearing right again at another gate, follow the narrow path into a wood and continue to a kissing gate with a Footpath arrow and the instruction to "Have Dogs on Lead".

Go through the kissing gate into a very wide avenue of really old beech trees and follow the path between them. As you progress, you will see the remains of Eastbury House over on your right. Only the converted stable block still exists but, by its size you can imagine how vast the whole House must have been. Actually, I can tell you - Sir John Vanbrugh (designer of Castle Howard) built Eastbury House for Lord Melcombe, who was born George Bubb (a Weymouth chemist) but who took his uncle's name of Dodington when he died without issue. The "offices" were built by 1718 whilst the House was begun in 1724 and finished in 1738 at a cost of £140,000. The main body of the House was 144 ft by 95 ft, joined by arcades which formed the Great Court which was 160 ft wide inside by 210 ft from the House to the Court gate. The Offices either side of the House extended 133 ft each by 161 ft with Inner Courts of 161 ft by 80 ft each. Two other Courts of 50 ft square were attached onto either end of this already immense block, making a total frontage of 570 ft. Campbell's Vitruvius Britannicus says "The great portico is the most magnificent of its kind in England, the columns 3 ft in diameter. The canals are filled by pumps worked by horses and the gardens are very extensive (*5 miles around the park*), with vistas and plantations of trees, many 50 years old when moved here".

Now, continue along the avenue as far as the woods which come in from your right. Go over the stile in the fence, over against the LH hedge, and then follow the hedge to a Footpath-arrowed stile in the fence at the end of this hedge. Over the stile, turn right onto the wide, grassy, sheep track and follow it to its end. Cross over the tarmac track, which is a remnant of a Roman Road. and go over the Footpath-arrowed stile in the opposite hedge into the field with a RH, tree-lined hedge. Follow the hedge to the far corner and around for about 50 yards to a Footpath-signed stile over on the left. The long, high, bush-covered mound which you are circumnavigating is the Bronze-Age Chettle Long Barrow. In 1760, all remains were removed from the Barrow and re-interred when Lord Melcombe turned the site into a fashionable grotto. A strange event happened here about that time when, during a thunderstorm, a keeper took shelter in the grotto. About 20 sheep had the same idea but, on seeing the keeper, they stayed outside. They were struck by lightning and all but the one in the middle were killed. Lord Melcombe told the keepers to give the meat to the poor but it was inedible because the bones were shattered and the flesh was stuck to the bones.

Over the stile, turn right to join a soft, rough Bridleway which comes up from your left. Follow it for about 250 yards along the edge of this very long, coppice-edged field until it narrows and plunges into a brambly, bushy path with "Little Wood" on your left and broken iron railings of Eastbury Park in the bushes on your right.

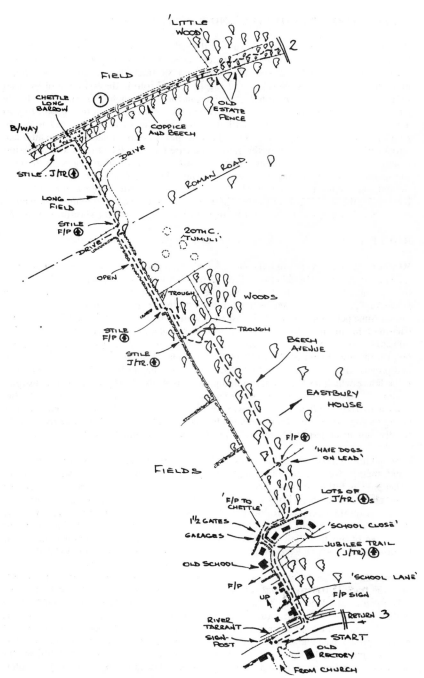

'LITTLE WOOD'

2

FIELD

CHETTLE LONG BARROW

① OLD ESTATE FENCE

B/WAY

COPPICE AND BEECH

DRIVE

STILE. J/tr.⊕

ROMAN ROAD.

LONG FIELD

STILE F/P ⊕

DRIVE

20TH C. 'TUMULI'

OPEN

TROUGH

WOODS

STILE F/P ⊕

TROUGH

BEECH AVENUE

STILE J/tr.⊕

EASTBURY HOUSE

F/P ⊕

'HAVE DOGS ON LEAD'

FIELDS

LOTS OF J/tr.⊕s

'F/P TO CHETTLE'

1½ GATES

GARAGES

'SCHOOL CLOSE'

JUBILEE TRAIL (J/tr.) ⊕

OLD SCHOOL

F/P

'SCHOOL LANE'

UP

F/P SIGN

RIVER TARRANT

RETURN 3

SIGN POST

START

OLD RECTORY

FROM CHURCH

STAGE 2

LITTLE WOOD TO CHETTLE AND EASTBURY FARM

With the vegetation reducing the width of the path, keep on going, past a LH "Private Woods" gate, until the track becomes wider. There are still snippets of iron railing in the RH hedge but this fence soon turns away and the track then disappears left into a more open part of Little Wood. Zig-zag Lt/Rt and follow the RH edge of the field until you arrive at a T-junction with a gate on the RH branch. Turn left onto the Bridleway which continues for 100 yards and then emerges from the woods to join another track which comes from your left. Bear right and follow the track to a farm gate and a half-gate - with a By-Way red arrow and a Jubilee Trail arrow - which lead into a parkland field. Aim for the gate in the wire fence on the other side of this field where a grassy track goes off into the LH corner to join another, more used track. Through this gate, you come into parkland where The Caravan Club may be found in the summer. Ahead of you, the RH edge of red-brick Chettle House comes into view but aim for the far LH corner of this field, towards a wooden gate where you have to decide whether to go all the way on **Route** 1 or to divert onto the shorter **Route 2.**

ROUTE 1: For the longer walk, go through the gate and turn straight to Stage 4

ROUTE 2: Don't go through the gate. Turn right about 20 yards before you get to it and head down the field between the LH wooden fence and the RH wire fence. In the dip, there is a farm gate whilst, over the LH fence, there is a fine view of Chettle House and part of the gardens which are open to visitors in the summer. The superb Queen Anne period house was built for the Head Ranger of Cranborne Chase, George Chafin on his marriage to Sir Anthony Sturt's daughter and they lived here from 1710 onwards. In 1755, George bought a plantation of fine Scotch firs in a 2 inches high box for the grand sum of 2/6d (12.1/2p) descendants of which still inhabit the park and provide timber for the Chettle timberyard which began in 1737. The fine, red-brick house which took 25 years to complete was probably the work of the designer of Smith's Square in London as both exhibit the unusual rounded corners. The last Chafin to live at Chettle House was William, born in 1732 and the eleventh of George's sons, of whom seven had already died. William, who died in 1818, was the locally famous author of "Notes and Anecdotes of Cranborne Chase".

Now, go through the gate by the wood and into a descending field beyond. There is a South-facing vineyard on your right. Follow the grassy track, with wire fences on either side, uphill to the next gate. Through the gate, there are trees in the track on your left and Thickthorn Long Barrow, excavated in 1700, on top of the hill on your right. After the next gate, follow the LH hedge as the path heads to a half-gate deep in the corner. Through the gate, the Footpath goes straight on (due South), across the corner of this field (but you may have to go anti-clockwise around the edge), to an un-arrowed stile which leads into a cleared area between two strips of woodland.

Go past this stile, down to the track which cuts through the strip of wood. Turn right onto the track (Bridleway) and follow it all the way to the top of the long field. When you meet a Bridleway T-junction, zig-zag rt/lt and, before the farm track begins to descend towards the farm, turn sharp right to follow the level, arrowed Bridleway along the top of the field against a LH hedge and fence. Follow the Bridleway, past a mobile 'phone mast and a water tank, to a farm gate in the far LH corner of the field. Go through the gate onto a T-junction of Bridleways, turn left and follow the descending Bridleway/track with trees both sides and deep undergrowth on your right.

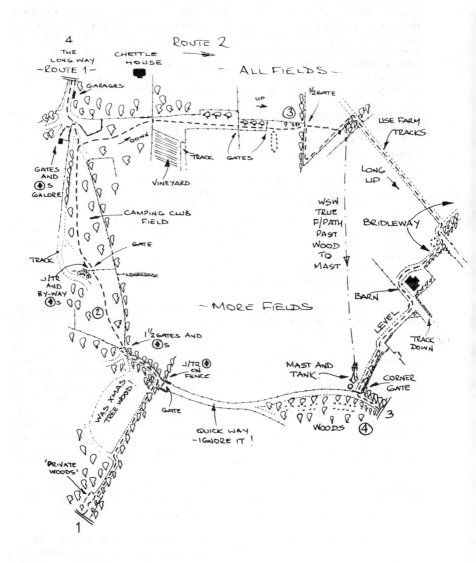

4
THE
LONG WAY
-ROUTE 1-

CHETTLE
HOUSE

ROUTE 2

GARAGES

- ALL FIELDS -

UP

½ GATE

③

USE FARM
TRACKS

DOWN

TRACK   GATES

LONG
UP

GATES
AND
④S
GALORE

VINEYARD

WSW
TRUE
F/PATH
PAST
WOOD
TO
MAST

BRIDLEWAY

CAMPING CLUB
FIELD

GATE

TRACK

J/TR
AND
BY-WAY
④S

②

- MORE FIELDS -

BARN

LEVEL

TRACK
DOWN

1½ GATES AND
④S

J/TR ④
ON
FENCE

MAST AND
TANK

CORNER
GATE

WAS XMAS
TREE WOOD

GATE

QUICK WAY
-IGNORE IT !

WOODS

④

3

'PRIVATE
WOODS'

1

STAGE 3

EASTBURY FARM TO TARRANT GUNVILLE

Follow the chalky track with grass up the middle down between the tree-edged field on your left and the strip of mixed wood on your right.   As the track bends its way down, the LH row of old trees follows the top of an earth bank and, after a broken old gate on your right, the RH narrow wood contains a similar bank.   As the track bends left, you cross the (unmarked) line of the Roman Road from Badbury Rings which passes the edge of Ashmore and joins up with the Drovers' Road from Shaftesbury to Old Sarum (Salisbury).   Still descending between trees, you pass the cattle-gridded gateway to Eastbury Farmhouse on your left.   Here, the track becomes a tarmac lane.

On the way down, you have good views through the RH trees of a four-gabled white house within a brick and flint-walled garden and a narrow gate soon leads into the private parkland.   However, keep on down to the junction at the bottom where the Tarrant valley road zig-zags across these old tracks.

The fine, stone-pillared gateway on your right leads to the cattle-gridded and iron-fenced drive to the four-gabled house, "White Kennels".   Past the post-box on the corner, follow the valley road more or less straight on between the fenced field on your left and the iron-fenced beech wood on your right.   On the way back to Tarrant Gunville, be prepared to cross to whichever side of the road gives drivers the best view of you but enjoy the level stroll with lovely views ahead to the little church of St Mary's, Tarrant Gunville.   The young River Tarrant runs through the low field and, when you reach the "Tarrant Gunville" sign, you will find that it has joined you between the fence and the small fenced wood and garden on your left.

Passing the white-fenced entrance to the driveway around the far side of the Tarrant's pond on your right, you will see the River running under the road to come out by the thatched cottage opposite.   Carefully follow the road - no verges now - to the fine, stone-pillared entrance on your right which leads to Eastbury House.   This is the gateway where, in popular legend, *George Bubb-Dodington's steward, William Doggett, waits for the coach to collect him and take him back to Eastbury House at midnight.*   Not much unusual about that except that *Doggett shot himself in the library when he was discovered appropriating materials during the building of the House.   The coach is driven by a headless coachman and pulled by headless horses and, when Doggett gets back to the library, he shoots himself all over again.   When his grave was in the way of the 1843-45 restoration of St Mary's, his body was found to be in perfect condition.   The preservation of Doggett's body caused local people to believe that he had become a vampire* but I wouldn't concern yourself too much over any of this.   The house was finished in 1738, Dodington died in 1762 and William died in 1786, 48 years after the House was finished, and there is a mass of other evidence to disprove the allegations against poor William Doggett.   All of this is fully detailed and explained in "Dead Interesting Dorset" ISBN 0 9519376 6 9.

Now, continue past the stone, flint and rendered house behind the wall on your left, which was once the "Bugle Horn Inn" (from the coat-of-arms of Lord Melcombe), and follow the iron-railed park back to School Lane and the T-junction beyond.   A visit to St Mary's would finish the walk very pleasantly and you really should see the lovely painted walls and organ .   The stone and flint church was built in 1503 but it was much restored in 1845.   Inside, there is a memorial to Thomas Wedgwood, son of the more famous Josiah Wedgwood, potter of Etruria, Staffordshire.

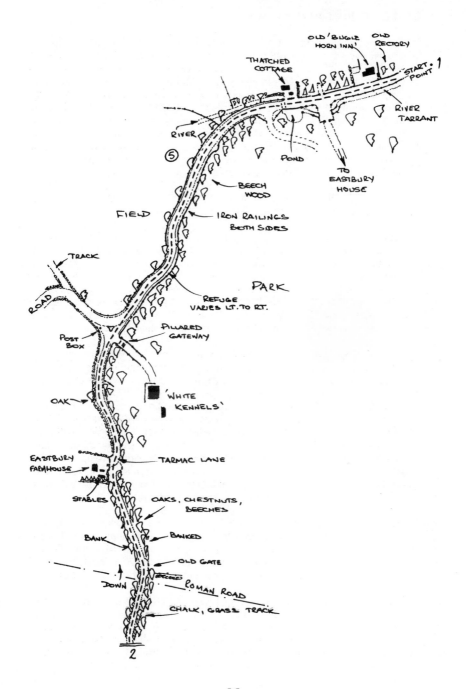

OLD 'BUGLE
HORN INN'

OLD
RECTORY

THATCHED
COTTAGE

START
POINT

1

RIVER
TARRANT

RIVER

⑤

POND

TO
EASTBURY
HOUSE

BEECH
WOOD

FIELD

IRON RAILINGS
BOTH SIDES

TRACK

PARK

ROAD

REFUGE
VARIES LT. TO RT.

PILLARED
GATEWAY

POST
BOX

OAK

'WHITE
KENNELS'

EASTBURY
FARMHOUSE

TARMAC LANE

STABLES

OAKS, CHESTNUTS,
BEECHES

BANK

BANKED

OLD GATE

DOWN

ROMAN ROAD

CHALK, GRASS TRACK

2

STAGE 4

CHETTLE TO PITT-RIVERS MUSEUM

Past the garages on your right and the entrance to Chettle Garden Centre, the lane continues past the drive to Chettle House and the private side gate in the low brick wall. Now, on the left, there may be either an old orchard or a 30 bay caravan park depending upon the outcome of a Planning Application. Our path turns left here onto the Jubilee Trail-marked footpath between this orchard/park and woods on the right but first, let's visit St Mary's Church, Chettle. In Old English, *Cietel* means 'a deep valley between hills' and, with the foundation of a monastery at nearby Cranborne about AD 930, Chettle was made a missionary centre by the Benedictine monks. The earliest recorded church here was built in the 14thC and three bells made in Salisbury in 1350 hang in the existing early 16thC tower. Alterations were made during the Stuart period but extensive rebuilding took place in 1849 after years of neglect and decay, similar to that endured by Chettle House whose restoration began in 1846 by its new owner, Edward Castleman. Memorials inside the church include fine marble tablets to members of the Chafin family, earlier owners of Chettle House.

Now, back on the Footpath - follow the bends and cross a track, which leads into an area of barns, onto the opposite path between a RH paddock and a LH hedged field. This path leads past garages and barns onto the road by a J/Tr and Footpath post. Turn left onto the road and go past the large barn on your left. After the three-gabled brick house on your left, turn right at the pair of cottages with the flint boundary wall onto the flint track with J/Tr and Bridleway arrows. Up this track, between hedges and a few trees, go past a LH turn and a RH house with another track to the right. Your grassy track continues up with a RH tree-verged fence and a LH fence.

You soon arrive at a pair of large gates straddling your track. As you cross the space between them, the fields open out on either side. Keep straight on, between a LH banked hedge and a RH banked fence, descending slightly. At the end of the enclosed track, by an electric wires support post and another J/Tr arrow, the path narrows and continues up the RH edge of a large, open and breezy field with fine views over fields and woods as you reach a pair of cattle troughs astride your path. Go through the pair of half-gates in the RH corner hedge and, on the other side, you get a view of the General Pitt-Rivers Museum which, until quite recently, housed the unique archaeological collection of this great Dorset barrows investigator. Keep following the hedge across this next long field, past a J/Tr arrow near a RH gate, to another "Public Bridleway" post by the half-gate in the far corner. Go through the gate onto the road and turn left, ignoring the Bridleway over on your right.

Follow the road, between banked hedges, past a row of houses on your right and, after the turning to Jay Cottage, the hedge and trees on your right attempt to hide Eltham House - the old Pitt-Rivers Museum and, before that, a short-lived Gypsy School which was begun in 1845, the year of the death of its founder, John West, Rector of Farnham from 1835 and missionary to the settlers and Indians of North America.

Now, immediately after the far entrance to Eltham Court, look for the Footpath-arrowed stile in the hedge over the RH bank. From this stile, the official Footpath heads diagonally to the visible farm gate in the LH hedge and then returns at a right-angle to the far RH corner. This should be your route but, if the worn path alongside the RH hedge is still existing when you arrive, go that way instead. It is in the right direction for our purposes and will save trampling on crops or meadow grass.

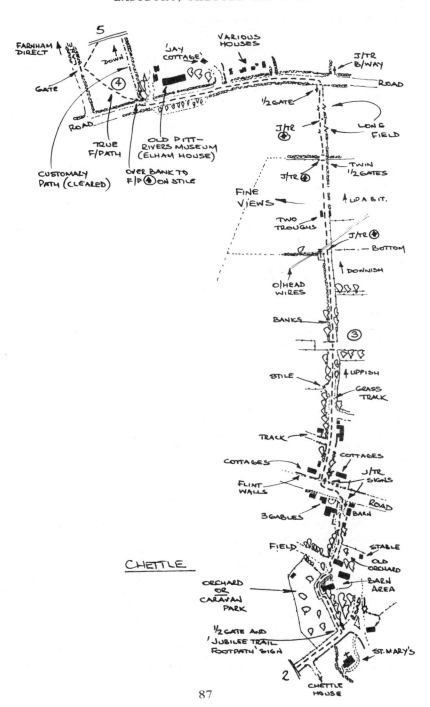

STAGE 5

PITT-RIVERS MUSEUM TO FARNHAM

At the bottom RH corner of the field, go over the J/Tr-arrowed stile onto a short, narrow path leading to another stile.   Over this stile, follow the top RH hedge to another pair of stiles, this time with Footpath arrows.   Over the stiles, follow the top hedge with a high field behind it on your right.   Down your field, on the left, you will see a small brick cottage but, when the RH hedge runs out, pay more attention to your line across the widening field ahead.   Aim for the RH end of the sub-station beyond the hedge and you will find a pair of stiles in the hedge.   Go over the stiles and down the steps in the bank into the high-hedged, descending lane.

Turn left to go past the cottage which you saw from the top field, now seen to be "Rose Cottage".   Then, after the lane comes back from Minchington on your right, go past the gate into the LH woods and past the high cob wall which encloses the RH barns.   Past the RH thatched house with the iron fence and the thatched garage, turn left onto the lane with the old corrugated-iron barns and the steel tube-protected ditch on the left.   A gate leads into the field with large chestnut trees whilst on your left is the thatched brick and flint farmhouse of "South Farm".   Keep on along the lane, passing brick and flint cottages on either side and with the ditch still running along the LH side.   You soon reach a T-junction with a Playground on the LH corner and with a ditch running under the road to the RH side where it meets a sign pointing to "Chettle, Tollard Royal and Minchington, Ashmore and Shaftesbury".

Turn left at the "Museum Hotel" and you will see that the road divides again - one way with a rough verge and a telephone box on the left and the other, narrower RH branch passing the Hotel's car park and a lovely brick and flint cottage before an apparent lych gate on the far LH corner.   With the LH trees hiding the view, I thought I'd found the church but I was surprised to find a cottage on the other side.   Closer inspection revealed that the thatched shelter was protecting an ancient village well and that the church was up the RH track.   So, turn up the hedged track and you will find the lovely Church of St Laurence standing behind the twin iron gates facing you. This is a pleasant, small, light church, built of green-grey Shaftesbury sandstone and flint and retaining its 14thC tower.   Inside, there are twin boards with gilt lettering bearing the Ten Commandments from Exodus XX - as there are at St Mary's, Chettle. Here, just inside the door, there is also a list of rectors dating back to 1291.

Leaving the church, turn up the narrow track , past the overflow cemetery on your right, to a stile with a choice of two Footpath directions.   One leads diagonally left up the field but ours follows the RH fence to another stile which faces you in the wire fence.   Go over the stile with the Footpath arrow and descend alongside the RH hedge to the bottom corner of the sloping field.   Follow the path round to the left, behind hedges and gates of houses which line the road to Tollard Royal.   After the houses, the hedge becomes mixed hedge and fence as you pass an enclosed clump of new trees on your left.   Before the triple barn, turn right and go down the short track, between a LH hedge and a RH wooden fence, to the road.   Turn left and walk up, between "Franklyn" on your left and a thatched cottage on your right.   Immediately turn left and go up the narrow path, between St Catherine's Chapel (1865) and a wood-fenced garden, to a Footpath-arrowed stile in the hedge.   Now, carefully find the line of the Footpath up this vast field as it is much too big to fight your way around the edge. An electric line crosses the top of the field on single posts, except the RH one which is a double post.   The target is 5 yards to the right of the last single post.   Go for it!

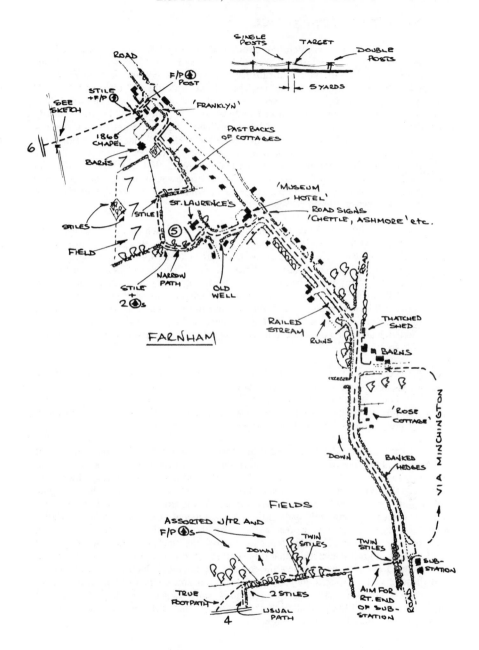

SINGLE POSTS

TARGET

DOUBLE POSTS

5 YARDS

ROAD

F/P ④ POST

STILE + F/P ④

SEE SKETCH

'FRANKLYN'

6

1865 CHAPEL

PAST BACKS OF COTTAGES

BARNS

'MUSEUM HOTEL'

STILE

STILES

ST. LAURENCE'S

ROAD SIGNS 'CHETTLE, ASHMORE' etc.

FIELD

⑤

NARROW PATH

STILE + 2 ④s

OLD WELL

FARNHAM

RAILED STREAM

RUINS

THATCHED SHED

BARNS

'ROSE COTTAGE'

DOWN

BANKED HEDGES

VIA MINCHINGTON

FIELDS

ASSORTED J/TR AND F/P ④s

DOWN

TWIN STILES

TWIN STILES

SUB-STATION

TRUE FOOTPATH

2 STILES

USUAL PATH

AIM FOR RT. END OF SUB-STATION

ROAD

4

STAGE 6

FARNHAM TO HATT'S COPPICE

Toiling up the field, you will perceive a section of wooden fence in the top LH corner. Go through the gap on its left and you will find a satisfying Footpath arrow on the other side. Go into the lane and turn right, passing the cottage on your right and following the hedged, banked lane past the entrance into the RH trees and to a RH bend with "Silver Birches" facing you. Turn left here onto a LH verged tarmac lane with a track on the right and banked hedges on both sides as it begins a steady descent. There is a lovely view of Farnham Woods on your right as you reach a narrow wood on the left of the lane. Reaching the bottom of the lane, you find the walled and gated entrance to "Hookswood Farm" with a neat lawn outside. Follow the lane straight on across the valley bottom, alongside the RH wire fence, and begin to ascend a narrow, horse-frequented track with no Bridleway arrows. There are good views across the field on your right all the way up whilst the LH trees shelter the long gardens of Hookswood Farm cottage.

At the top of the hill, the fence runs out just before you reach an un-arrowed gate in the tree-enhanced fence across your path. Turn right after the gate and follow the cleared track alongside the RH fence on high, airy Chettle Down (now fields) with fine views on your left over South Cranborne Chase. The fence-enclosed hollow of bushes and the gulley which cause the path to deviate along here are remains of an ancient "Settlement" and, although the land is extensively farmed, slight humps and bumps can still be seen around the clump of small trees. There is, or was, a pile of old tree trunks at the bend in the Bridleway ahead and it provided an excellent place for a sandwich and a cup of coffee amid thoughts of those who lived their lives in this beautiful spot.

Another pleasing aspect of this field is its significance as a prime example of the maintenance of Public Rights of Way (I hope this is still true). Unlike some areas which we have found, the Bridleway along the edge of this field is cleared and wide and the Bridleway across its centre is a perfect width and is smooth and grassy from many years of preservation. Many thanks to whoever is responsible.

Now, at the dual Bridleway-arrowed posts, turn left and descend to the junction of Bridleways at the foot of the field. Ignore the track which goes straight up beyond the gate facing you. Instead, turn right onto another cleared track which runs alongside the low LH hedge. At the end of this green track, go through the farm gate into a wide, open, grassy area with a grass track coming from a gateway down on your left, crossing your path and heading up into the ancient oaks and beeches of Hatt's Coppice. Don't go into the woods but bear slightly left to find the dirt track which runs parallel with the LH valley fence. Follow the track between the hedge and Hatt's Coppice until you can see that it is bearing off to a gate over on your far right. You should leave it now and follow the edge of the coppice which now stands on the left ahead of you. Go past the gate which leads into this coppice and head for the far LH corner of your low field. Before you go, I heard a cuckoo in Hatt's Coppice on April 26th. I don't know whether that was early or whether I'd missed Letters to the Editor of The Times by a matter of weeks.

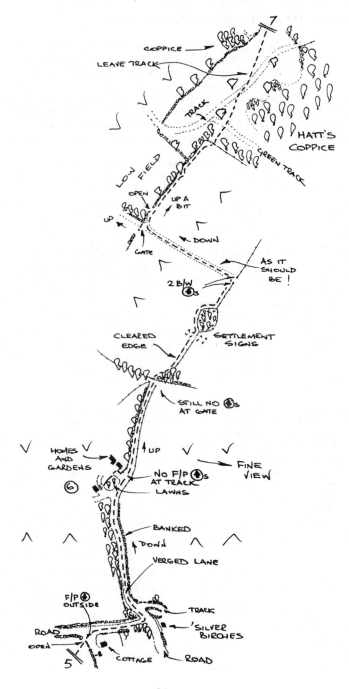

STAGE 7

HATT'S COPPICE TO MARLBOROUGH LANE

Still aiming into the far LH corner, to the junction of the coppice and the tree-lined wire fence ahead of you, you will find entrances into the field after the coppice and into a hedged, flint, chalk and grass Bridleway.   Join the triple-lane track - You know, two for tractor wheels and a middle one for horses - and follow it, slightly ascending, for about 1/4 mile.   After a farm gate, the track bends gently right and left to take you through a farmyard area with brick and flint barns enclosed by a similar high wall on your right whilst the farmhouse hides behind high hedges on your left. This is Green Close Farm - abandoned and very sorry for itself at the time of writing.

Anyway, keep following the bending track, with a LH hedge and with the overgrown coppice (and bluebells if the time is right) of Downend Coppice on your right.   At the end of the track, upright steel joists stop vehicles from approaching Green Close Farm whilst there is a gate along the track on your right which leads into the woods. You have arrived at Bloody Shard Gate which leads into Bloodway Coppice.   On December 16th 1780, this was the scene of one of the bloodiest battles between the Cranborne Chase keepers and a group of poachers, the leader of whom was a trumpet major by the name of Blandford.   Both sides were heavily armed and serious injuries were equally imparted, one of the keepers dying later from his wounds.   In his "Anecdotes and History of Cranborne Chase" of 1818, William Chafin recalled that one of Blandford's hands was severed and he was saved from bleeding to death by the quick first aid actions of the keepers and by Mr Dansey, the surgeon, who dressed his wound the next day.   At the poachers' trial in Dorchester, they were sentenced to transportation for seven years but, such were their wounds, this was commuted to imprisonment.   Later, Blandford was made to retire from the army with a pension and he set up a shop in London selling - of all things - game.   His hand had been buried in Pimperne churchyard and, as Blandford was buried without it, it is reputed to wander the lane at night desperately trying to find him.   Let's go.

Turn left and follow the track away from the gate, past a solitary tree on a small grassy island on your right, before a corrugated iron barn, and join the wide, chalky track at a gate and a Bridleway arrow on the adjacent fence.   At the top of the track, just before you begin a slight descent, you cross the line of the Roman Road from Badbury Rings to the Drovers' Road junction near Shaftesbury.   Descend to the crossroads where the tarmac lane comes up from Tarrant Gunville straight ahead and turns down to Busseys Stool Farm on your right.   Turn left onto the uphill gravel track with the LH verge and wire fence and a row of pines on the right.   A short track turns right at the end of the pines but keep straight on, now with a high LH field and with fine views on your right.   At the top of the rise, go through a plethora of gates with cowsheds on your right followed by an arrowed crossing of Bridleways with a gate to the track on your right and a level track running between hedges on your left.

Keep straight on for another 1/4 mile, with fine views all around, until you arrive at the edge of a wood of old oaks after the track has skirted past some water pumping sheds.   The track straight ahead has joined the Roman Road but don't follow it. Instead, turn right through the Footpath-arrowed gate and follow the wide track down between the LH woods and the RH hedge and fence.   At the end of the wood, the track becomes the most wonderful, soft, grassy, descent between wide hedges with views towards the Eastbury avenue and St Mary's, Tarrant Gunville.   So, just keep on down and enjoy the exhilarating stroll.

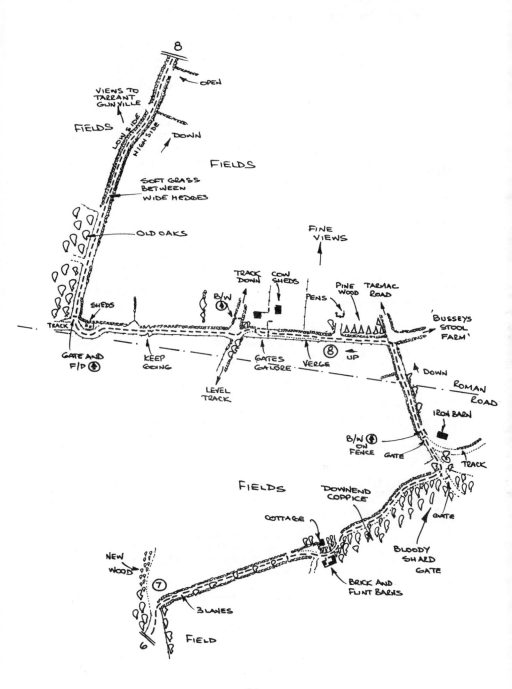

8

OPEN

VIEWS TO
TARRANT
GUNVILLE

FIELDS

LOW SIDE
HIGH SIDE

DOWN

FIELDS

SOFT GRASS
BETWEEN
WIDE HEDGES

OLD OAKS

FINE
VIEWS

TRACK
DOWN

COW
SHEDS

PENS

PINE
WOOD

TARMAC
ROAD

B/W

SHEDS

'BUSSEYS
STOOL
FARM'

TRACK

GATE AND
F/D

KEEP
GOING

GATES
GALORE

VERGE

8

UP

DOWN

ROMAN
ROAD

LEVEL
TRACK

IRON BARN

B/W
ON
FENCE

GATE

TRACK

FIELDS

DOWNEND
COPPICE

GATE

COTTAGE

BLOODY
SHARD
GATE

NEW
WOOD

7

BRICK AND
FLINT BARNS

3 LANES

FIELD

6

MARLBOROUGH LANE TO TARRANT GUNVILLE

Still descending pleasantly on soft grass between hedges, you eventually arrive at a gate and a stile across your path.   Go over the unmarked stile and pass gates into a field and the old Marlborough Farm barns, now a small industrial estate, on your left. With a LH verge, the lane has become tarmacced as you continue down towards journey's end.

Passing a bungalow and a row of pines on your left and entrances to two houses' drives on your right, you reach the fine, brick and flint "Barn House" on the bottom LH corner.   After such a long time in the outback, take care as you tread onto the road opposite Chine Cottage and turn left.   Make sure there is no traffic coming and cross over to the right side of the road with the infant, or dry, Tarrant running along the ditch between the fenced road and the field beyond.   The fine, three-storeyed brick, stone and flint house over on your left is Marlborough Farmhouse.

Now, keep straight on, passing Old Home Cottage, where the Tarrant crosses over to the left.   The more modern Tarrant Gunville seems to have been built on the left of the road with plots of bungalows and estate houses whilst there are still fields behind the thatched, brick and flint cottages and barns on the right.   After the Village Hall on the left and the telephone box by the Old Post Office on the right, you arrive at a row of flint cottages beyond their long front gardens and the next thatched house on the RH corner brings you back to the T-junction where you started your walk.

It would be a shame not to pay a visit to St Mary's whilst you are here so turn right up the hill (signposted for Everly Hill) and you'll find the pathway which leads to it over on your left.   If you've already been on *The Cranborne Chase Path*, you'll probably have been here before but it's still worth a visit.   This low, stone and flint church with its typically squat tower, was built in 1503 but extensively rebuilt, enlarged and consecrated October 2nd 1845.   The decoration on the walls and ceiling in the chancel were done about 50 years later, reflecting the influence of the Oxford Movement.   There is a memorial inside to Thomas Wedgwood, son of the more famous Josiah Wedgwood, potter of Etruria, Staffs.   Thomas was a pioneer in the field of photography who succeeded in creating an image but was unable to "fix" the pictures and they faded very quickly.

One more thing before you go home.   On the outside chancel wall, to the right of the porch, there is a memorial to Sir Thomas Dacombe, Rector 1549, carved into the stone.   The inscription reads:

HERE LITHE S T D PARSON
ALL FOWRE BE BUT ONE;
EARTH, FLESCHE, WORME AND BONE
MCCCCCLXVII

True - but a trifle morbid.   Perhaps it's time to go home and remember the sunnier aspects of this superb walk.

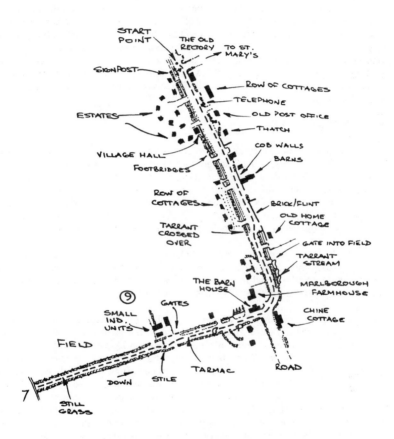

START
POINT

THE OLD
RECTORY

TO ST.
MARY'S

SIGNPOST

ROW OF COTTAGES

TELEPHONE

OLD POST OFFICE

ESTATES

THATCH

COB WALLS

VILLAGE HALL

BARNS

FOOTBRIDGES

ROW OF
COTTAGES

BRICK/FLINT

OLD HOME
COTTAGE

TARRANT
CROSSED
OVER

GATE INTO FIELD

TARRANT
STREAM

THE BARN
HOUSE

MARLBOROUGH
FARMHOUSE

⑨

GATES

SMALL
IND.
UNITS

CHINE
COTTAGE

FIELD

TARMAC

ROAD

7

DOWN

STILE

STILL
GRASS

PART FIVE - WINTERBORNE WONDERS

INTRODUCTION

No. It's not a mistake and, when you follow these *wander*ings, you'll know why. I know it's been said many times before but this walk really is something very special. When I finished the longest option, I felt exhilerated, knowing that I'd been treated to a beautiful microcosm of inland Dorset, I'd revelled in high downs rambling with views to the distant coast and with the best view of beautiful Milton Abbey (from the elevated 12thC St Catherine's Chapel). I had enjoyed three beautiful streamside villages and their lovely churches and been treated to a stroll through superb ancient woods with bluebells and wild garlic - well, it was late spring - together with the sight of a lovely, stone manor house and its old tithe barn. Such treats, all encompassed in a mere 10.1/2 miles of alternating breezy and sheltered walking. One of two Winterborne valleys in Dorset, the stream rises in Winterborne Houghton and trickles down to Winterborne Stickland and, growing bolder, runs through Winterborne Clenston on its way to join the River Stour. *Wonder* full countryside and a sheer treat.

THE ALTERNATIVES

The residential area not far from the top end of the reputedly most beautiful street in Dorset at Milton Abbas is used as the starting point for both options because there are more available parking places and there are more buses to Milton Abbas than to any of the other lovely villages that we visit. Local bus No. 111 stops frequently at the street called Catherine's Well (which leads straight to St Catherine's Chapel) so use this street as your start and finish - at Reference ST809022 on OS Map No. 194. Park very thoughtfully in Catherine's Well if you aren't using the public transport.

Whilst both Routes begin and end in Catherine's Well, the only difference is that Route 2 returns through a different section of the vast Milton Abbey Wood but it misses out on a valley stroll to visit the Manor House, the ancient tithe barn and the beautiful St Nicholas' church at Winterborne Clenston.

ROUTE 1: Total distance 10.1/2 miles. This option begins with a visit to St Catherine's Chapel in Pigeon House Plantation with a most beautiful view of Milton Abbey below and, after a stroll on breezy Houghton Down, the path descends in a charming hollow-way into Winterborne Houghton where the Winterborne stream first appears, just before St Andrew's church. An easy field path leads past watercress beds (now a trout farm) into Winterborne Stickland where we visit the lovely St Mary's church. You can then enjoy an easy country lane amble alongside the Winterborne to the Manor House, tithe barn and charming St Nicholas' church in Winterborne Clenston. The return begins through the lovely mixed trees of Oatclose Wood with bluebells, wild garlic, foxgloves and ferns, depending on the season, and then follows Footpaths over high farmland, finally emerging into the lovely street of thatched cottages in Milton Abbas, by the 18thC St James' church.

ROUTE 2: Total distance 7.3/4 miles. This Route differs from Route 1 only by its decision to cut short the circuit at Winterborne Stickland and to return directly to Milton Abbas by way of Charity Wood - still as beautiful as Oatclose Wood on Route 2 but shorter. Actually, this is the wood which reminds me so much of my favourite forest - Whinlatter Pass in the Lake District. Leaving the woods, a short lane delivers you into Catherine's Well without visiting the picturesque main street.

STAGE MILEAGES

STAGE	MILES	TOTAL MILES

ROUTE 1:

1 Milton Abbas to Stone Lodge	1	1
2 Stone Lodge to Higher Houghton	1.25	2.25
3 Higher Houghton to Watercress Beds	1.50	3.75
4 Watercress Beds to Quarleston Farm	1.50	5.25
5 Quarleston Farm to Winterborne Clenston and Oatclose Wood	2	7.25
6 Oatclose Wood to Hoggen Down	1.50	8.75
7 Hoggen Down to Milton Abbas	1.75	10.50

ROUTE 2:

1 to 3 As above from Milton Abbas to Watercress Beds	3.75	3.75
4 Watercress Beds to Stickland Fields	1.50	5.25
8 Stickland Fields to Milton Abbas	2.50	7.75

Tithe Barn, Winterborne Clenston

97

WINTERBORNE WONDERS ROUTE LAYOUT

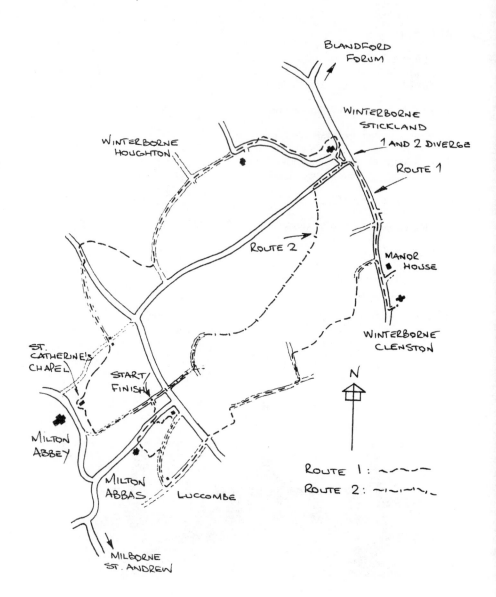

Labels within the map:
- BLANDFORD FORUM
- WINTERBORNE STICKLAND
- 1 AND 2 DIVERGE
- ROUTE 1
- WINTERBORNE HOUGHTON
- ROUTE 2
- MANOR HOUSE
- WINTERBORNE CLENSTON
- ST. CATHERINE'S CHAPEL
- START FINISH
- N
- MILTON ABBEY
- MILTON ABBAS
- LUCCOMBE
- ROUTE 1: ~~~~
- ROUTE 2: ~·~·~·~
- MILBORNE ST. ANDREW

The Abbey Church of Milton Abbas

Doorway to St Catherine's Chapel, Milton Abbas

STAGE 1

MILTON ABBAS TO STONE LODGE

Starting by the "Jubilee Trail" and "Footpath" signs on the slip-road island, follow the pavement down Catherine's Well, past Sylvan Row on your left and Gravel Road over on your right, until it becomes a wide, flinty track with grass verges.   Milton Abbas village nestles below the sloping field on your left but the hillside is too steep for you to see even the chimneys of the thatched cottages.   Never mind - you'll see them on the way back if you stay the full course.   There are fine distant views ahead as the track descends slightly and begins to narrow between hedges and a couple of farm gates, some iron railings and a cattle trough on the left.   A bank of rhododendrons and some species trees on the corners of a private driveway accompany you on a downhill bend into the start of Pigeon House Plantation.   A couple of faint paths turn into the trees on your right but keep descending for a few more yards until you find a forest track on your right, opposite a barn yard.   The sign with its back to you says "12thC Chapel 1st on Left" whilst the Hilton road appears straight ahead.   Turn up this chalky forest track and go right around the barrier.

Follow the levelling track between mainly beeches until, after another LH path, the track bends right to go round the back of the simple, flint and stone buttressed St Catherine's Chapel.   Leave the track and walk to the LH end of the chapel where you will find a bench seat.   On your way, note the fine studded door and the strong, Norman arch around the stone infill which reduced the doorway to its present size. The inscription on the left of the doorway "grants indulgence of 120 days to pilrims stopping here".   If the door is unlocked, go inside.   It's like stepping back a couple of centuries.   The old wooden forms, seats and lectern are dusty and mouldy, as are all of the walls.   The chapel was used as a dovecote by the monks of the Abbey (was that the basis of the name "Pigeon House Wood?) and, after that, it was converted into a labourer's cottage by Lord Milton, Earl of Dorchester.   Restored in 1967, the chapel affords a glorious bird's eye view of Milton Abbey at the foot of over a hundred turf steps (which look like a grass slope from here).

Drag yourself away from this almost perfect view and continue along the path, around the left of the next barrier which proclaims that "Forest Enterprise Welcomes Walkers".   After a short, steep stroll on a peaty, flinty path, you rejoin the wider track and continue uphill with odd paths and tracks going up into the woods on your right and down into a steep combe on your left.   Keep going up as the track bends and you will notice a dry-stone wall over on your right.   This is the boundary wall of the deer park and it runs to Nursery Cottage Farm.   Several more tracks turn down steeply on your left and, if it's the right time of the year, you should see carpets of bluebells before the ferns emerge into frond-waving life.   After a grass track turns off right towards the farm, another barrier leads you out onto a junction of tracks.   The right turn heads back to the farm.   The instant left, valley-entrained track is King Edward's Drive which, if followed through the twin gates of Stone Lodge and across the upper Bulbarrow road, continues as a narrowing Bridleway down into Charity Wood along a section known as Lady Damer's Drive.   Caroline Damer was the widow of George Damer, the second Lord Dorchester who died in 1808, and she ruled Milton Abbas estate until 1828 when it passed to her cousin, Lord Portarlington.

Now, bearing left, pass across King Edward's Drive and in front of Stone Lodge. Follow the wide track with a wire fence on your left and the garden hedge on your right up, around one last barrier towards the pine-lined drive ahead.

2

UP

DRIVE

STONE LODGE

'KING EDWARD'S
DRIVE'

DOWN

GRASS TRACK

1

NURSERY COTTAGE
FARM

UP

DRY-STONE
WALLS

WALKERS
WELCOME

MILTON
ABBEY

QUITE STEEP

ST CATHERINE'S
CHAPEL

BARRIER

PIGEON HOUSE
PLANTATION

'TO
CHAPEL'

BARN

UP

BEECHES,
SYCAMORES

TRACK

PATHS

DOWN

RHODODENDRONS

TROUGH

LOW
FIELD

HIGH
FIELD

VERGE

MILTON
ABBAS

GRAVEL ROAD

SYLVAN
ROW

ROUTE 2
RETURN

STEPS

J/Tr. F/PATH
SIGN

START

TELEPHONE

'CATHERINE'S WELL'

RETURN—
ROUTE 1

STAGE 2

STONE LODGE TO HIGHER HOUGHTON

After the pine-lined forest track comes in from your left, keep following the level track straight on for about 1/2 mile with the deer park wall beginning to fall down over on the right. Bluebells and garlic thrive in Haydon Plantation amongst the tall, old oaks which stand behind the bordering pines and hazel bushes. At a left turning grass track, your route descends slowly, passes a green open area, bends a couple of times with grass verges on both sides and then, after a track turns left by a Forest Enterprise notice, deposits you at a barrier with a Bridleway arrow post outside.

In this wide entrance, with fenced woodland on your left and a Bridleway turning off through bushes into the deer park on your right, carefully wander out into the road and turn left. Cross over and follow the RH, tree-lined edge of Bulbarrow Road, now with an open-floored coppice on your side, until you find 1.1/2 gates leading into the RH field (Houghton Down Gate). A Bridleway post indicates your direction (vaguely) but follow me. You are just entering the top fields of Houghton Down at a height of 685 ft above sea level and the long-distant views all around are superb. However, cut across the corner of the coppice (Clump 1) and head towards the LH end of the next, smaller bush and scrub patch (Clump 2). From here, the same slightly descending direction would take you to an even smaller clump (Clump 3) but, on your way, you will stumble across a wide grass track which emanates from a gate out of Bully Plantation over on your left. Turn right onto this track and keep in an ESE direction - the left, faint fork when the track divides and, for further confirmation, you will be descending slightly whilst the right fork stays level. You should see a tall communications pylon in the distance, directly ahead.

With patches of hawthorn and some hazel bushes scattered about the downs, keep straight on, slightly downwards and eventually passing wire-fenced hawthorn bushes on your left, towards a gate in a sunken track down in the far LH corner. When you reach the end of the open downs, drop down into the steep-sided track and turn down it to the gate where you will find a Bridleway arrow post and another gate into the field on its left. On the other side of your RH gate, there are two painted Bridleway arrows. One points up the track and the other points in the direction of your arrival.

Carefully walk down the high bank-enclosed, flinty and chalky track with grass up the middle. It's quite steep and smooth so it can be slippery when wet *and* slippery when dry. The bank on your left is higher than that on your right. In fact, there is a deep valley head appearing on the right. There are good views to Winterborne Houghton and that pylon when the RH trees give way to wire fencing.

After a coppice on your left and a gate into the field on your right, the track begins to level out on your approach to Higher Houghton Farm corner.

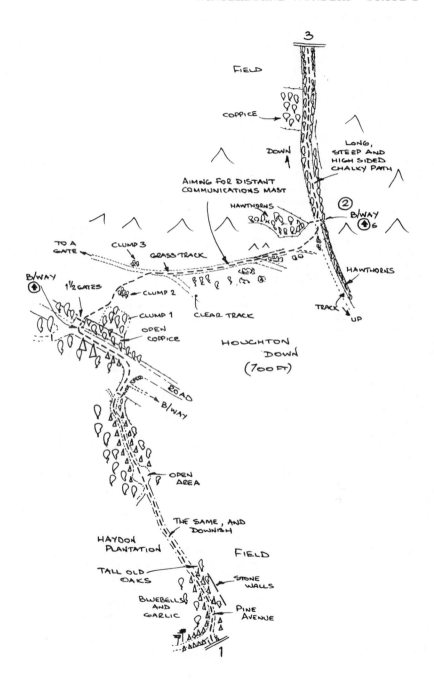

FIELD

COPPICE

DOWN

LONG,
STEEP AND
HIGH SIDED
CHALKY PATH

AIMING FOR DISTANT
COMMUNICATIONS MAST

HAWTHORNS

② B/WAY
S

TO A
GATE

CLUMP 3

GRASS TRACK

HAWTHORNS

B/WAY

1½ GATES

CLUMP 2

CLUMP 1

OPEN
COPPICE

CLEAR TRACK

TRACK

UP

HOUGHTON
DOWN
(700 FT)

ROAD

B/WAY

OPEN
AREA

THE SAME, AND
DOWNISH

HAYDON
PLANTATION

FIELD

TALL OLD
OAKS

STONE
WALLS

BLUEBELLS
AND
GARLIC

PINE
AVENUE

1

STAGE 3

HIGHER HOUGHTON TO WATERCRESS BEDS

When you reach a cross-roads at the hedged end of the Bridleway, a track goes off to the farm buildings on your right and a tarmac farm road runs up the valley bottom to "Higher Houghton Only" on your left. On the LH corner, you will find wooden Bridleway arrows pointing to "Ibberton" along the farm road and to "Milton Abbas" back up the track behind you.

Keep straight on into Winterborne Houghton village, with high hedges soon giving way to rows of hedged and lovely front-gardened cottages with the infant Winterborne stream running as a ditch on the RH side. A Footpath turns off before the thatched Manor Cottage on your right but follow the road until you come to a T-junction with the LH turning signposted to "Bulbarrow 2.3/4". Here, you will find a bench commemorating 100 years of the Parish Council in 1995 and a telephone box. On the opposite corner, behind the hedge, stands Pound Cottage. This would be referring to the site of the village pound where lost and strayed cattle were taken to the hayward who kept them until the owner claimed them and paid the accepted fee. The fenced area opposite seems about the right size for a pound. Beyond that fenced area, you will see the stone and flint St Andrew's church. Continue down the road, signposted for "Winterborne Stickland", and turn up the next RH driveway (half of which leads to The Old Rectory) to visit the church.

Standing on the site of the Early English church of about 1250, originally dedicated to both St Mary and St Andrew, the present church was rebuilt in 1862, re-using some of the old stone, whilst the East wall of the chancel and the South wall of the nave are probably the oldest remaining parts. The three bells in the tower are of widely varying ages - one is dated 1717, one is dated 1596 and the oldest is probably 14thC, cast at the medieval foundry in Salisbury. There are some intriguing notices inside including a complete list of priests from John de Dentone in 1316 and Roger, succentor of Sarum *sans date* before him, the Ten Commandments from Exodus XX and a wooden plaque which outlines the condition for a grant of £75 from the Incorporated Society for Buildings and Churches in 1862. It says that 174 free seats "numbered 1-23 and 32-39 are to be reserved for the poorer inhabitants of this parish" Numbers 1-23 clearly refer to the pew numbers in the main body of the church but I couldn't find pews 32-39. Actually, Number 1 isn't there now, either.

Leaving St Andrew's, continue along the road, passing more cottages, Glebe Farm and Dunbury Farmhouse on the right and Welcombe House on the left, opposite which is the start of the trout farm where watercress beds once thrived on the clear, chalky waters of the Winterborne. There are hedges on both sides now but, after a long barn appears in a LH field and before you reach the end of the trout farm, turn left up a wide, hedged gravel track. This is a Bridleway - which continues straight through the gate facing you and up the field on the other side - but you need to turn sharp right at the Footpath arrow, between the LH wire fence and the RH garden hedge.

Go over the Footpath-arrowed stile and follow the clear path across the low level of this field with a wire fence running along the skyline up on your left. Go through the next gate and follow the same path through this very long field, parallel with the road. On the other side of the road, the trout farm soon runs out and the Winterborne becomes a real stream with wild watercress growing in it.

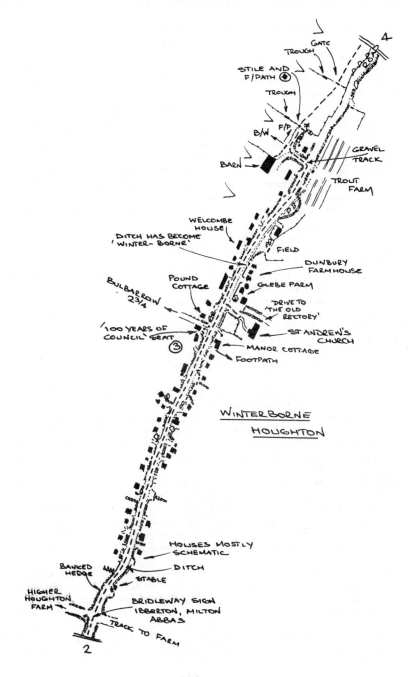

STAGE 4

WATERCRESS BEDS TO QUARLESTON FARM or STICKLAND FIELDS

At the end of this long, sloping field, go over the Footpath-arrowed stile and follow the edge of the next field, against the row of garden fences which border the houses and cottages lining the road into Winterborne Stickland. Two paths turn off to the road as you wander along the path but keep straight on for a few yards more. Now look across the field for the stanchions which hold the overhead electric cables. You will notice that one which stands up on your left carries a barrel-shaped switchgear box whilst one up and over the rise carries a square switchgear box. Cut across the corner, aiming for this square one, and you will arrive at exactly the right spot for the exit stile from this field. Climb over into a descending track between hedges with a bungalow on your left and garages and the British Legion H Q on your right. At the bottom of this track, you emerge into North Street, Winterborne Stickland between a thatched cottage on the left and a row of twin-gabled Victorian brick cottages on your right. A signpost confirms that it is 1 mile back to Winterborne Houghton. With "Joy's Cottage" opposite, turn right and follow North Street past a long row of brick cottages on your right and a row of continuous thatched cottages over on your left.

After "The Shire Horse" public house, the chapel and the War Memorial, just before the village shop, bear right around the corner into West Street. The road sign shows the way to several villages en route to Blandford Forum and Milton Abbas. Follow West Street as far as a right turn, by the Post Office, which leads to the Parish Church of St Mary the Virgin. Built originally in the 13thC, the church and its revenues were sold to Milton Abbey in 1336. The chancel is the original 13thC construction with a carefully restored 16thC wagon roof. The nave and the piscina in the South wall, near to where a second altar would have stood, are also 13thC. Some of the roof timbers and bosses have been painted in the typical bright fashion of the Middle Ages. The 15thC tower contains four bells - three 17thC bells and a 'new' treble bell dated 1905. There are more details in the church leaflet and I entreat you to buy one.

Leaving the church, by the 16thC porch with its unusual double-sundial, cross over the road into the third side of the triangle opposite, past the ancient lime tree in the centre. Keep straight on along this short road to the complicated junction ahead. Now it's decision time. Do you want to go and see Winterborne Clenston's lovely church, the 16thC Manor House and the ancient, vast tithe barn (Route 2) or save yourself 2.3/4 miles by taking the quicker way back to Milton Abbas (Route 1)?

ROUTE 1: Turn right up the lane past Dunbury School on your left. Continue up the hedged and banked lane until you reach the Bridleway-signed LH turning into the gated track through Valley View Farm's barns. Past the barns, go through the D C C-arrowed gate and follow the direction of the arrow, bearing half-right to cross the valley in this wide field at an angle, aiming for the junction of hedges in the far right corner on the other side of the valley. Then turn to Stage 8.

ROUTE 2: Continue along Clenston Road after the chain-bordered village green with its benches and its 1977 Jubilee village cross. Past the RH turning by The Old Malt House, carry on along the hedged, un-verged lane with the Winterborne joining you for a while and with assorted bungalows and houses behind the banked LH hedges. After the stone and flint Quarleston Farm with its entourage of new courtyard cottages on the right, past Quarleston Hamlet and a Bridleway-signed track by the twin 1901 cottages on the left, ignore the Bridleway sign after the hidden stile on your right.

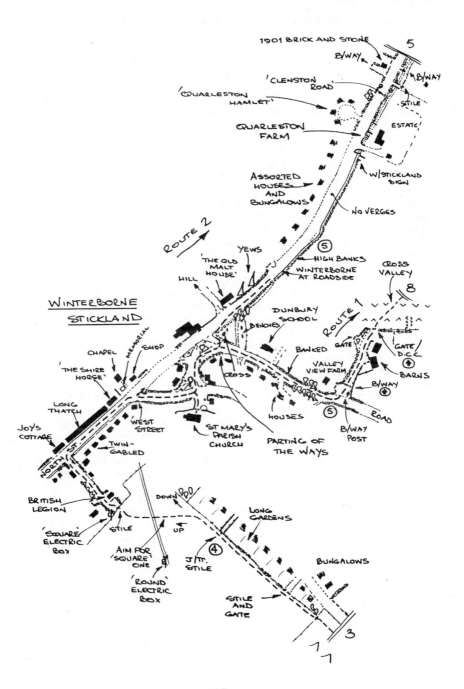

STAGE 5

QUARLESTON FARM TO WINTERBORNE CLENSTON
and OATCLOSE WOOD

The Winterborne, having run behind the hedge at Quarleston Farm, now turns round the back of "The Old Tithe", thatched cottage and wooden barn on your right. The high walls and the two wooden gates on the verged LH side of the bending road protect the old barns of Skelder House, the fine house which stands behind the next pair of gates and the high hedge. On your right, the Winterborne appears again behind a wooden fence just turning under a brick bridge to the LH side of the road .

A little further along the road, a track turns right, opposite a bus stop. After a driveway to a row of cottages, a second track turns right before a garage in the low field behind the hedge on your left. Still following the long, level and hedged road, you next pass some flint stables behind a cob wall, immediately followed by "The Old Rectory" and a wide verge with a telephone box around the corner. Follow this verge past the first left drive and past the long, brick, flint and stone barn behind the wall. Then, whilst trying to see the superb late 15thC to early 16thC mullioned Clenston Manor House through the twin-gated entrance, take note of the Bridleway-arrowed, track on your right. You'll want this track after you've seen St Nicholas' church.

Now, on the LH corner, there stands an enormous flint barn with huge porches like church transepts. It has a chequer-board pattern clay tiled roof and window slits whilst, inside and out of view, it has a hammer beam roof which is so sturdy and ecclesiastical that it has been suggested it may have come from Milton Abbey, to which it belonged. However, tithe barn roofs were commonly built in the same way as church roofs. Why have two different designs for the same structural purpose? After the barn and the Bridleway for Blandford St Mary which turns left towards the far row of four cottages, follow the fenced road around the sweeping bend with an unusual high-windowed house over on your left. You soon arrive at the drive on the left, past a cob and flint cottage, to St Nicholas' church. Here is the Winterborne again - under the bridge at the end of the drive. This lovely little church, with the ogee-headed arch over the spired tower door and its blue-painted and gold-starred chancel ceiling, was built in 1840. Here, too, are the Ten Commandments, either side of the altar.

Return now to the Bridleway which you saw near the tithe barn and turn left onto the rising track, with trees on your left and the wire-fenced field on your right, and go round the barrier. Follow the bending track into Oatclose Wood, now with oaks and beeches on both sides, past a garage and a woodland cottage with Victorian cast-iron windows on your right. The track is now grassy and, past the next barrier, becomes narrower - through a wood carpetted with bluebells in May. In this world of Dutch elm disease, I was delighted to find wych elms flourishing in these woods - they're the tall trees with barks like sand-papered oaks and with circular seed wings.

From here, enjoy the woodland stroll but don't get lost. After crossing a very faint path, keep on until you reach a division into three paths. You want the centre path - a faint blue arrow exists on the moss-covered tree on its RH corner. Join this path and follow it, level to very slightly upward, and continue for quite a way, around some fallen pines unless they've been moved, and across a track crossing (more faint blue arrows). After bearing right, your path suddenly turns left, with another path backing right, to find a Bridleway arrow on the post of the gate leading into the high field outside the woods. Turn right onto the wood and fence-enclosed, grassy track.

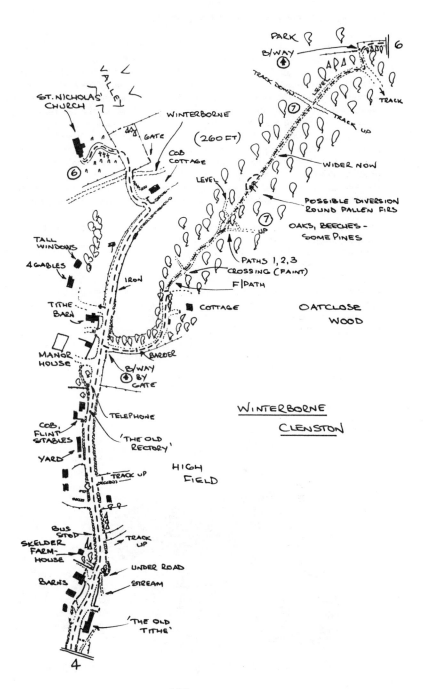

PARK

B/WAY

TRACK DOWN

LEVEL

TRACK

TRACK UP

ST. NICHOLAS' CHURCH

VALLEY

WINTERBORNE

GATE

(260 FT)

COB COTTAGE

LEVEL

WIDER NOW

POSSIBLE DIVERSION ROUND FALLEN FIRS

OAKS, BEECHES - SOME PINES

TALL WINDOWS

4 GABLES

IRON

PATHS 1, 2, 3 CROSSING (FAINT)

F/PATH

TITHE BARN

COTTAGE

OATCLOSE WOOD

MANOR HOUSE

BARDER

B/WAY BY GATE

TELEPHONE

WINTERBORNE CLENSTON

COB, FLINT STABLES

'THE OLD RECTORY'

YARD

TRACK UP

HIGH FIELD

BUS STOP

SKELDER FARM-HOUSE

TRACK UP

UNDER ROAD

BARNS

STREAM

'THE OLD TITHE'

4

STAGE 6

OATCLOSE WOOD TO HOGGEN DOWN

You are now out in the open, near the end of the ridge which follows the Winterborne valley, and about to descend into a parallel, short valley but, before you go, enjoy the long views as far as the Dorset coastal ridges from the Purbeck hills to Chaldon Down, near Weymouth. Now, walk down the steep grassy track, with Oatclose Wood on your right and the slopes of Whatcombe Common on your left, past a half-gate sized opening and weaving around encroaching bramble patches, to find a half-gate at the bottom. A faint track heads up into the mostly thin beeches of Cliff Woods on the opposite side of this valley but Bridleway arrows ensure that you turn left and follow the '3-lane' track along the valley floor. After 1/4 mile of easy, slightly downhill strolling, you arrive at a Bridleway-arrowed barrier which opens onto a wide junction of tracks. Turn right, with scots pines on the RH corner and a sign for "Milton Park Wood", and go around the barrier onto a forest track with grass up the middle through the woods with pines on your left and beeches on your right.

After a short stroll, a narrow track bears off to the left whilst the main track continues upwards towards a more open area. Take the narrower track, which resembles a river bed, up to an open gateway with two Bridleway arrows on the post. Do *not* head up the valley straight ahead but turn instantly left to go up the steep, cleared edge of the field for about 300 yards. When you reach the top, do not go through the hedge into the next field but turn right onto the cleared Bridleway, keeping the hedge on your left and with views to Barnes Hill Farm across the valley on your right. This is an easy, level path for about 1/4 mile until you arrive, after a long hedgeless gap, at a pair of farm gates. This is Hoggen Down and there are excellent views to the coast from this high, breezy spot, as well. However, you're well on the way to finishing this grand walk, so go through the gates into the tractor pull-in area and then carefully cross the road into the grass verged entrance and descending gravel track to "Luccombe Farm Business and Craft Centre".

Better late then never - this is St Nicholas' church from Page 108

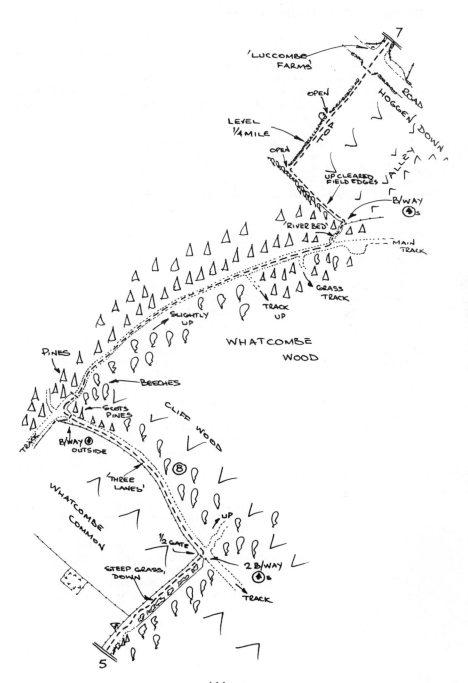

7

'LUCCOMBE FARMS'

ROAD

HOGGEN DOWN

OPEN

LEVEL ¼ MILE

TOP

OPEN

UP CLEARED FIELD EDGES

ALLEY

B/WAY ④s

'RIVER BED'

MAIN TRACK

GRASS TRACK

TRACK UP

SLIGHTLY UP

WHATCOMBE WOOD

PINES

BEECHES

SCOTS PINES

CLIFF WOOD

B/WAY ⑧ OUTSIDE

'THREE LANES'

⑧

WHATCOMBE COMMON

UP

½ GATE

2 B/WAY ④s

STEEP GRASS DOWN

TRACK

5

STAGE 7

HOGGEN DOWN TO MILTON ABBAS

Keep down the flinty track to the Riding Centre and the Craft Centre units on the right with their 'doughnut' pond on your left, and the fenced East Luccombe Farmhouse. Now begin to ascend, past openings in the hedges on left and right and past a RH gate and LH cattle trough. At the top, you pass a pair of cottages just before a Footpath turns off left at a farm gate onto a hedged track. Ignore this path but turn right at the gate after the cottage gardens, onto a wide, Jubilee Trail-arrowed track which runs between a new, narrow wood and the pine wood which surrounds the two cottages.

The track zig-zags where a track returns into the pine woods behind you on your right and an opening leads into the RH field. Keep following this high track between the new LH wood and the RH hawthorn hedge, past a pair of gates into adjacent fields on your right and past another J/Tr arrow. After a horse-jump on the right and after the new wood has finished on your left, you arrive at a short wooden fence with a J/Tr arrow pointing straight on. If you're desperate to get back, and don't want to visit beautiful Milton Abbas, St James' church or the "Hambro Arms", keep straight on and follow the Path 2 directions. I'm not going to miss anything. Coming with me?

Path 1: Turn left off the track and follow the cleared, undulating field edge alongside the LH hedge until you reach the end of a small wood on the LH corner. Now turn sharp right and walk straight up and over Luccombe Down, through any crops unless the path has been cleared. On the other side of the ridge, you descend to a Footpath-arrowed stile in a wire fence, over which you cross a narrow field to another Footpath-arrowed stile into the steep beech woods with a wire fence on your left. These woods line the top end of Milton Abbas village. Down the very steep path, ignore the path which turns right - it only leads to the top-enders route. Keep on down and you will find yourself on the edge of a precipice which drops into the rear of St James' church. This Gothic style church was built for the displaced villagers when Joseph Damer, Lord Milton, 'landscaped' the original village. The sprawling cottages which had grown around the Abbey over the years spoiled the view from his home so he used several devices, some legal and some simply lack of maintenance, to have them removed. He had the present, admittedly delightful, village or 'new town' completed by 1791 whilst St James' was dedicated in 1786. After visiting the church, walk up the hill, past or via the "Hambro Arms", past Dunbury First School on your left and past the Footpath-signed steps on the right. Here is where the top-enders come out so we're all together again at "Paths 1 and 2" below.

Path 2: Keep following the track until it bends right, passing a narrow, fenced path to the top road, through a small RH wood. Don't go all the way to the road gate or down the track to the barn but bear left (directed by J/Tr and Footpath arrows) along the fence which encloses the barn area. At the end of the wire-fenced enclosure, bear left and pick up a faint grass track which runs parallel to the beech woods on your right. Take the first J/Tr and Footpath-arrowed stile in the RH fence and follow the wending, but well-arrowed, path down through the trees to some steps into the top end of Milton Abbas and turn right. The Path 1 walkers meet you here.

Paths 1 and 2: Follow the pavement past some large Victorian brick houses to a signed, narrow Bridleway and, through the wooden chicane, walk up the steep, woody and bending path to the top where you emerge onto the last few yards to your starting point shown on the Stage 1 map.

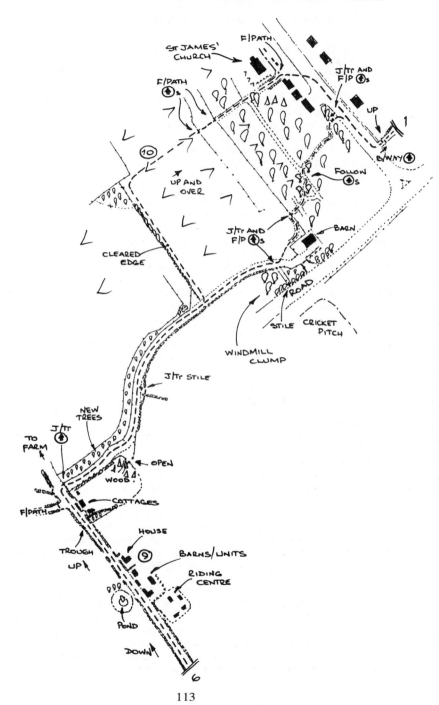

STAGE 8

STICKLAND FIELDS TO MILTON ABBAS

When you arrive in the corner, go through the Jubilee Trail-signed half-gate into the steep field and keep to the rising footpath next to the RH hedge.   At the top of this field, go through the fence-protected gateway into the next large field and join a wide path going to the right.   This soon turns left on top of a raised track bisecting two open fields and heads off towards the woods on the other side.   Reaching the other side, the path bears right and leads you to a gate next to a short piece of wooden fence.   Go through the gate into Charity Wood and, in spring or early summer, you'll find the woods filled with bluebells or foxgloves on both sides of the grassy path. This is part of Whatcombe Wood of which Milton Park Wood forms another section. In Hutchins History and Antiquities of Dorset, it is recorded that, about 1793, "three pairs of roe-deer *Capreolus Cervus* were introduced into the Milton Abbey Woods by Lord Dorchester, one pair from the North of England, and the rest from America, and so well did the situation and climate suit them, that their descendants are now to be met with over a considerable tract of country".

This is a vast wood with many tracks crossing or leaving your route but don't turn left or right unless I tell you and I'll get you through alright.   Keep straight on as a you join a wider trackcoming in from the right.   Shortly, you will find yourself passing between some wonderful, stately, ancient, and vastly spreading, beech trees after which the track descends slightly to a right bend with two tracks turning off on the left.   J/Tr and Bridleway marker posts stand on the opposite corners as you bend right into a due-West direction.   Keep descending to the bottom of a dip, where a J/Tr-marked track turns off to the left, and then ascend a steep slope.   A few yards after the top of the slope, an even wider gravel track comes in from your right to join your 'straight-on' route.   The track is now long. level, gravel and easy with a left sweep and the start of a descent.   At the very next right sweep of the main track, look left and you'll see a narrow path descending into the woods at a J/Tr and Bridleway arrow post.   The quickest way is down this narrow path, bending on a downhill slope, until you emerge and turn left back onto the main track on the other side of this hairpin wood.   However, if you want to stay in the open, just follow the main track down around a right sweep, a left bend, another right sweep and a left hairpin to find the narrow path coming out of the woods on your left about 100 yards down the track. If you kept to the track, you will have passed a faint blue painted arrowed path going off to the right at the hairpin.   This was where Lady Damer's Drive came out into Milton ParkWoods after the drive from Stone Lodge which we passed earlier today.

Well, now that we're all together again where the narrow path comes out to join the main track, keep on down for a few yards and turn right at another J/Tr and Bridleway arrow post.   This leads you into a narrow, steeply rising, loose path.   Go up this path and you soon have a wire-fenced field on your right, tree roots in your path and a grassy track going off to your left opposite a field gate.

At the top of this narrow path, still with fields on your right, start a steep descent to the forest track at the bottom where you will find a wide gate across the track on your left and confirmation Bridleway and J/Tr arrows on the gatepost.   Turn right and follow the left hairpin bend between mixed trees again.   On a right, uphill bend, you leave the forest and continue, past a paddock on your left and again on your right, to join the wide, hedge-lined tarmac lane to the cross roads into Catherine's Well on the Stage 1 map, passing Hill House and Keeper's Cottage on your way.

114

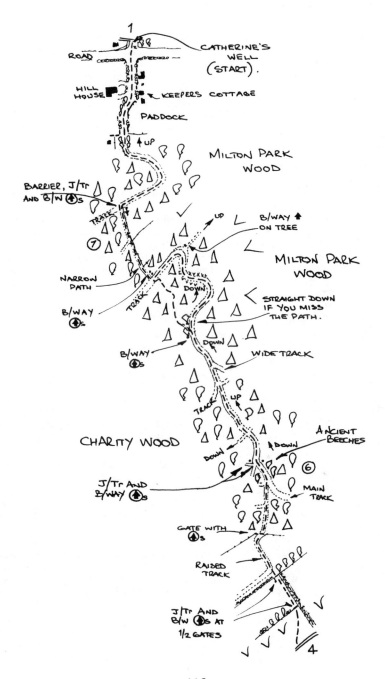

1

ROAD

CATHERINE'S WELL (START).

HILL HOUSE

KEEPERS COTTAGE

PADDOCK

↑UP

MILTON PARK WOOD

BARRIER, J/Tr AND B/W Ⓐs

TRACK

UP

B/WAY ↑ ON TREE

MILTON PARK WOOD

⑦

NARROW PATH

DOWN

STRAIGHT DOWN IF YOU MISS THE PATH.

B/WAY Ⓐs

B/WAY Ⓐs

DOWN

WIDE TRACK

TRACK

UP

CHARITY WOOD

ANCIENT BEECHES

DOWN

DOWN

⑥

J/Tr AND B/WAY Ⓐs

MAIN TRACK

GATE WITH Ⓐs

RAISED TRACK

J/Tr AND B/W Ⓐs AT ½ GATES

4

PART SIX - SWANAGE AND PURBECK

INTRODUCTION

All Dorset lovers know Swanage and many will have walked some of the Coast Path and the ridges overlooking Swanage already but not many walkers have explored the valley between the ridges or the abandoned stone-mining area behind the popular coastal paths. So I have devised several routes to visit the best medieval farmland, Purbeck stone cottages, a fine Manor House in the foothills of Nine Barrow Down and an ancient wood. We walk the uniquely landscaped downland which resulted from the old Purbeck stone workings, a quarrymen's village with several places of refreshment and a house made famous by its role in the D-Day landings. Most Routes end with a high, breezy cliff-top walk back to Swanage.

THE ALTERNATIVES

Starting and finishing outside the Tourist Information Centre on Swanage seafront - Reference SZ031790 on O S Map No. 195 - two Routes head straight out of town for Godlingston Manor and Knitson Farm. From there, they turn South to the National Trust's Wilkswood mixed woodland, the village of Langton Matravers and Spyway Barn. Alternative returns either follow Priests Way over ancient tracks and through old stone-mining sites to Swanage or down to the cliff-face quarries at Dancing Ledge and along the Coast Path, past Anvil Point lighthouse and through a lovely woodland walk. The two other Routes follow Priests Way from Swanage to Spyway Barn and return along the cliff-top Coast Path.

ROUTE 1: Total distance 11 miles. From the Tourist Information Centre, the Route leads straight out of town, parallel with the restored steam railway line, and through valley fields to the 14thC Godlingston Manor House. A country lane then leads to Knitson Farm in the midst of 14thC strip fields and over undulating meadows to ancient Wilkswood. A visit to Langton Matravers' Parish Church of St George's and possibly a quarrymen's watering hole, is followed by a stroll from the village to the cliffs where the stone was won, passing Spyway Barn on the way. After an exploration of Dancing Ledge, an undulating, breezy walk along the cliff-top Coast Path brings you to Durlston Country Park, Anvil Point lighthouse and the Victorian Trail along wooded cliffs into Swanage with superb panoramic views on your arrival.

ROUTE 4: Total distance 9 miles. This Route differs from Route 1 by turning off at Spyway Barn and missing the Coast Path but enjoying a walk along Priests Way on the farmed and mined inland side of the hills which overlook your outward journey and which enjoy lovely views of Swanage, its surrounding ridges, Swanage Bay and the Isle of Wight. You return past the Cottage Hospital and the Town Hall with its elegant front elevation, built for the Mercers' Hall in London in the 17thC.

ROUTE 2: Total distance 8 miles. Whilst still beginning at Tourist Information, this Route follows Swanage Bay into town before leaving by the roads, the high tracks and the Priests Way which is used by the returning Route 4. Reaching Spyway Barn, this Route turns coastwards and shares the Coast Path with the Route 1 walkers.

ROUTE 3: Total distance 9.1/2 miles. This is exactly as Route 2 but it diverts to visit Langton Matravers and passes the grounds of Leeson House, still guarded by the concrete gun-posts which signify its importance in World War II. It joins Route 1 for the walk past Spyway Barn to the Coast Path and the return to Swanage.

STAGE MILEAGES

STAGE	MILES	TOTAL MILES
ROUTE 1:		
1 Swanage to Prospect Fields	1	1
2 Prospect Fields to Knitson Lane	1.25	2.25
3 Knitson Lane to Windmill Knap	1.25	3.50
4 Windmill Knap to Wilkswood	1	4.50
5 Wilkswood to Langton House	1	5.50
6 Langton House to Spyway Farm	.50	6
7 Spyway Farm to Blackers Hole	2	8
8 Blackers Hole to Anvil Point	1	9
9 Anvil Point to Peveril Down	1.50	10.50
10/1A Peveril Down to Swanage	.50	11
ROUTE 4:		
1 - 6 As Route 1 to Spyway Farm and Putlake Barn	6.50	6.50
3A Putlake Barn to Belle Vue Lane	.75	7.25
2A Belle Vue Lane to Townsend Heights	.50	7.75
10/1A Townsend Heights to Swanage	1.25	9
ROUTE 2:		
10/1A - 3A Swanage to Putlake Barn	2.50	2.50
6 Putlake Barn to Spyway Farm	.50	3
7 - 10/1A As Route 1 return to Swanage	5	8
ROUTE 3:		
10/1A - 2A As Route 2 to South Barn	2	2
3A South Barn to Leeson Fields	.25	2.25
5 Leeson Fields to Langton House	1.75	4
6 - 10/1A As Route 1 return to Swanage	5.50	9.50

SWANAGE AND PURBECK ROUTE LAYOUT

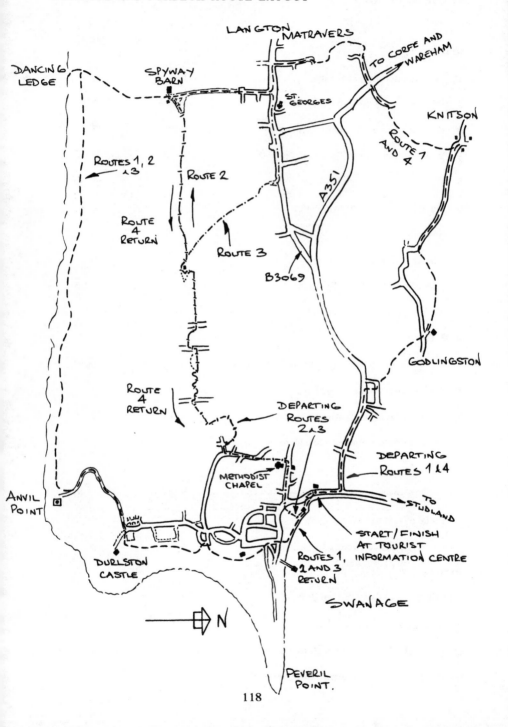

Stone mine winch, Durlston Country Park, Purbeck

Godlingston Farm near Swanage

119

STAGE 1

SWANAGE TO PROSPECT FIELDS

Swanage is a lovely old-style seaside town with a distinctly Victorian air.   Listed in the Domesday Book as both *Sonwich* and *Swanwic*, held by Walter Thunder from the Countess of Boulogne, wife of Hugh FitzGrip, Swanage clearly is of ancient origin as are Herston on its Western border and Godlingston.   Most of Swanage's buildings are of the local Purbeck stone and many are roofed with it as well.   At its height, Swanage was shipping 50,000 tons of stone annually and sold 15,000 tons (50 ship loads) for the construction of Ramsgate Harbour.   The Victorian houses are mostly red-brick with Welsh slate because rail transport had made access to these cheaper materials much easier by then.   Towards the end of the 18thC, William Morton Pitt of Kingston Maurward near Dorchester began the tourist industry here, converting the old Manor House near the Stone Pier at the foot of Seymer Hill into an hotel, later "The Victoria" after the Queen's visit on 25th Oct. 1835.   The face of Swanage was changed forever by the joint efforts of the Mowlems and George Burt, one of the partners in the building company.   Mr Burt brought several London relics back to Swanage - not the usual insignificant souvenirs but vast stone edifices, cast iron bollards and lamp-posts.   Most notable are the front of the Town Hall which is the complete, richly embellished frontage made for the Mercers' Hall and the Clock Tower, not far from the gun batteries of 1774 at Peveril Point.   The tower was originally erected near London Bridge as a memorial to the Duke of Wellington .

Now, starting outside the old Purbeck stone and stone-slate roofed Tourist Information Centre which faces Swanage Bay, follow the line of bathing huts away from the town centre towards the recent stone jetty.   Turn up Victoria Avenue away from the sea and, after the pleasant gardens and the Catholic Church of the Holy Spirit and St Edward by the traffic lights, follow its suburban normality in the form of blocks of flats and rows of houses past King George's Fields and Forres Sports Field beyond the hedges on the left side of the road.   After about 1/2 mile, before Victoria Avenue begins to bear left for the bridge over the restored Swanage Steam Railway lines, look out for a narrow passageway which runs off between Nos. 84 and 86 - signed "Public Footpath to Northbrook Road".

Turn up the fenced passageway and, emerging into the top road of houses, turn left and look out for the next Footpath which runs off right between Nos. 30 and 32.   There isn't a Footpath sign but walk up between the wire fenced gardens to a stepless, unmarked stile at the top end.

Over the stile, the walk really begins and you have your first views of Nine Barrow Down, the ridge which runs between Swanage and Corfe Castle and which rises to its maximum height of 654 ft right ahead of you.   Don't worry.   You don't have to climb it on this walk.   You follow the broad, open and fertile valley of Wealden Beds to Knitson Farm.   However, bear left at the stile and walk down towards the LH end of the facing hedge with a wire fence on your left.   As you progress, you will see a path coming up from your left and heading down the next field towards the bottom left corner, through rough grass at about 350 degrees (almost due North).   Follow it down, ignoring the Footpath-arrowed stile in the LH hedge on the way.   Go through the low stone-posted gate in the hedged corner between a small oak tree on the left and dog-roses and elderberry bushes in the hedge on the right.   Now, follow the LH wire fence in this next field with Nine Barrow Down right in front of you and with the high downs and white cliffs of Ballard Down over on your right.

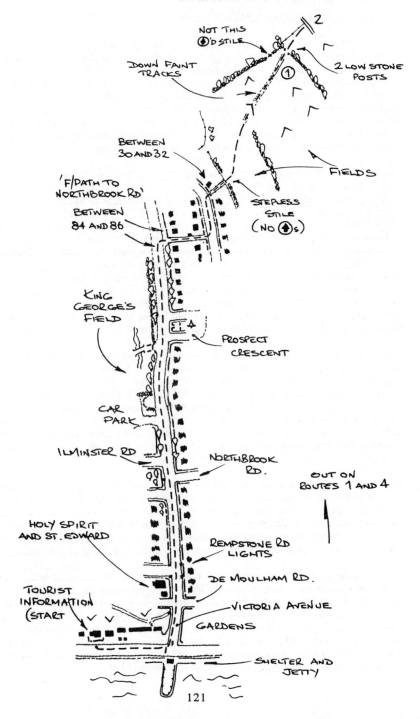

NOT THIS 🔄'D STILE

DOWN FAINT TRACKS

2 LOW STONE POSTS

①

②

FIELDS

BETWEEN 30 AND 32

'F/PATH TO NORTHBROOK RD'

BETWEEN 84 AND 86

STEPLESS STILE (NO 🔄s)

KING GEORGE'S FIELD

PROSPECT CRESCENT

CAR PARK

ILMINSTER RD

NORTHBROOK RD.

OUT ON ROUTES 1 AND 4

HOLY SPIRIT AND ST. EDWARD

REMPSTONE RD LIGHTS

DE MOULHAM RD.

TOURIST INFORMATION (START

VICTORIA AVENUE

GARDENS

SHELTER AND JETTY

121

STAGE 2

PROSPECT FIELDS TO KNITSON LANE

As the wire fence ends, a stile from the LH field brings another path to join you from Prospect Farm.   This time, bear down to your left and find the Footpath-arrowed, stepless stile over the ditch in the LH hedge, ignoring the other stile which is in the bottom corner of the field.   Over the stile, turn immediately right in the soft, red-soiled field of Wealden clay and walk anti-clockwise around the edge of this uphill field with a border of reeds and pre-historic horse-tails (*Equisetum*).   These modern horse-tails are the same as fossilised plants found in the coal measures of the Radstock area - only much smaller.   Their predecessors (*Calamites*) are millions of years old and formed trees up to 50 ft high in the tropical swamps.

Anyway, follow the RH ditch until you reach three rows of overhead electric wires. Turn right at the post with the Footpath arrows just before the second wires and follow the edge of the field along the RH reed-filled ditch, past gate posts and walking under two rows of overhead wires.   Near the top, the RH field is much lower and the wire fence bends around to meet the top high hedge.   Go over the arrowed stile in the hedge and cross the sleeper bridge, emerging onto the Ulwell to Knitson Road. Cross straight over to the stony farm track opposite, signed "Footpath. Godlingston Hill 1 and Corfe Castle 3.3/4".   Walk up the track with the wood-fenced field on your right and the banked barn-yard on your left.   The tourist route instantly turns right to Nine Barrow Down.   Before we go on, let me tell you what Hutchins says about *Nine Barrow Down*: "..in all *eighteen* barrows are clearly distinguishable, the largest being 64 ft dia by 30 ft high".   Don't turn off here but follow the track straight through the farmyard, passing Godlingston Manor in the stone-walled garden on your right.

Godlingston and *Moleham* were separate entries in the Domesday Book but *Moleham* is now just a parcel of land to the South of the farm.   It was held by Durandus the carpenter, a servant of the King, together with some land at *Wilcheswood*.   By 1412, Robert Rempston held lands and rents here (Remember his road by the traffic lights just as you started out?) and the Manor House was built around this time.   The deeds for the House date back to 1427.   It has a thick-walled round tower at the West end - probably built for defensive purposes - and originally had a high main hall.   Hugely altered in the 17thC, an upper floor was built above the hall and, following a fire in the 19thC, the interior was greatly remodelled.

Past the modern barns and the sturdy stone cottages and sheds, go through the gate with the yellow arrow painted on the fence post and into the next field which slopes uphill ahead of you and towards the foothills of Nine Barrow Down on your right. Follow the tractor track alongside the wire fence on your left to the cattle trough on the top.   From here, there are fine views back to Swanage and the sea and across the low valley to the chalk ridge on your left where you will be walking on your return.

Now, continue alongside the fence down to its end, where a tree-filled hedge runs down past another cattle-trough on your left and a wire fence goes uphill on your right.   If it's summer, there will be caravans beyond the hedge on the far side of this field but you need to find a gate which is in the far, low down, LH corner where the high hedges meet - on a bearing of 250 degrees, nearly due West.   Arriving at the gate, go through the gap on its LH side and you will find yourself on the Knitson lane, on a sharp bend.   There are trees and high hedges all around as you turn right and begin an easy, although uphill, stroll between banked fields.

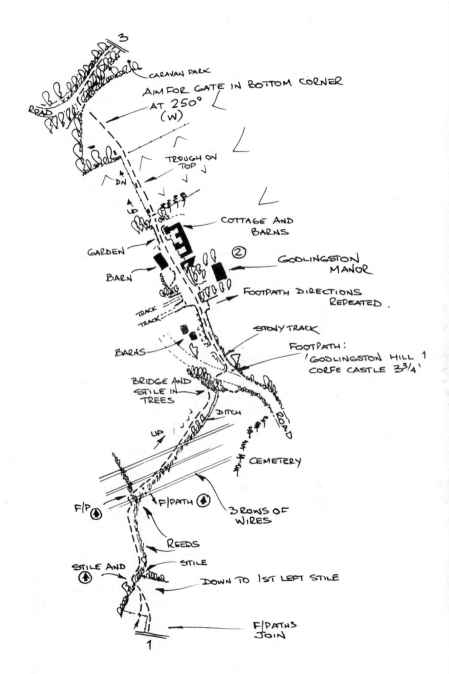

STAGE 3

KNITSON LANE TO WINDMILL KNAP

After the gate into Knitson Tourers Site (caravans) on your right, there are reasonable verges on either side but, past the bin area on your left and the track up to Knitson Naturist Field on the right, the road becomes contained below high banks and hedges as the gradient increases slightly.   With mainly beech hedges as you progress up the hill, you eventually arrive at a complicated wooden fence system on your right and a "Private. No Footpath" gate on the left.

This is the Knitson Farm complex and, before you turn down into the dairy yard immediately on your left (with a yellow painted arrow on the block wall adjacent to the road), walk along the road to have a look at the original Knitson Old Farmhouse. Don't go up the "Bridleway. Nine Barrow Down" - itself an ancient droveway - which passes its door but admire it from a more circumspect position near the road.   It is a low, Purbeck stone cottage with a fine, heavy stone roof and its garden is a picture in summer.   The cottage was built in 1634 although there were settlements and strip fields here centuries before that - the first recorded settlement being 1318.   In 1774, Hutchins merely described Knitson as "a hamlet and little farm in Afflington tithing" although he does explain how the estate passed between three branches of the Clavell family - the Clavells of Leston (Leeson), Steeple and Kimmeridge.   The latter would be the family which produced Sir William Clavell, the oil-shale, alum and glass entrepreneur of Kimmeridge and John Clavell, the builder of Clavell's Tower - see Encombe Encounter in "Dorset in a Fortnight" for further details.

Have a casual look at the Dairy Cottage and Knitson House, both 18thC but much altered, as you return to find the Footpath which descends to the milking shed down the gravel yard.   As you reach the shed, there is a "Footpath" sign on its wall directing you through the farm gate on the left, below a fenced bank.   Through the gate, follow the track round to the right, past a silo and a carousel steel fence where the cattle are directed into the milking shed.   Keep going round until you find a gate leading onto a downhill chalk and gravel track with fine views back to Swanage on your left and along the valley to Creech Hill and the chalk ridge beyond on your right.   Ignore the gates and fence sections between you and this gate because they are temporary and constantly changing positions.   Go through the gate and walk down the steep track, ignoring the branch which bears off to the right.   Go through the next gate with the painted yellow arrow onto a wide, grassy track between a RH wire fence and a row of hawthorns and struggling oaks, which used to be a hedge, on your left.   Level for a short distance, the track soon begins to rise towards a pair of gates. Go through the RH gate (no arrows) and follow the wire fence on your left to become entrained between a narrowing RH ferny bank and the original fence.   At the two hawthorn bushes on top of the low ridge, you can see St James' church, Kingston away on your right (at 260 degrees) in the trees on top of the much higher ridge.

Now, follow the RH wire fence to a stile with two Footpath arrows (on the other side). The Footpath which goes along the wire fence to your left follows the bottom edge of Windmill Knap, the summit of Coombe Hill where there really was a windmill in days gone by and where the flat top of the knoll is still slightly hollowed.   Instead of the swoosh of sails, the only sounds now are those of yellow-hammers and grasshoppers (in the summer).   Continue down the field, keeping to the RH hedge, passing between a hedge and reeds on your left and a sessile oak on your right.   You soon arrive at a low track which begins at a low oak on your right and a high bank on your left.

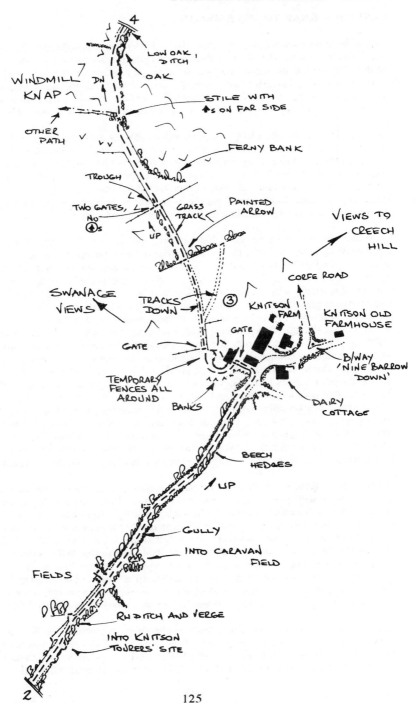

4

LOW OAK,
DITCH

OAK

WINDMILL
KNAP ↗   DN

STILE WITH
♠s ON FAR SIDE

OTHER
PATH   v   v v

FERNY BANK

TROUGH

TWO GATES,
NO
♠s

GRASS
TRACK

PAINTED
ARROW

VIEWS TO
CREECH
HILL

CORFE ROAD

SWANAGE
VIEWS

TRACKS
DOWN

③

KNITSON
FARM

KNITSON OLD
FARMHOUSE

GATE

GATE

B/WAY
'NINE BARROW
DOWN'

TEMPORARY
FENCES ALL
AROUND

BANKS

DAIRY
COTTAGE

BEECH
HEDGES

UP

GULLY

INTO CARAVAN
FIELD

FIELDS

RN DITCH AND VERGE

INTO KNITSON
TOURERS' SITE

2

STAGE 4

WINDMILL KNAP TO WILKSWOOD

Follow the grass track with the very deep, hedged ditch on your right and the edge of Windmill Knap on your left down to the farm gate which leads out of the field.   Walk up the stony track to the top where you meet a tarmac lane and an electricity post with a Footpath arrow.   There are many barns of various shapes and sizes all around whilst the best are of local Purbeck stone.   Turn left onto the lane and walk downhill past the "12' 6" Max Height" sign and past New Barn Farmhouse over on your right.

Go under the stone bridge which carries the restored Swanage Steam Railway track on its way to Corfe Castle.   If you're lucky, you may have a brief, pre-Beeching moment as a steam train thunders over your head.   Now, begin to climb up from the tree-lined lane and over the stream bridge.   This is the same stream which runs through King George's Playing Fields and out into Swanage Bay at the stone jetty where you set out earlier today.   Past "Little Acorn" pig sheds on your right, the lane climbs round to the right and soon emerges at a crossroads with the A351 Wareham to Swanage road.

Cross over the A351 into the shady, banked lane opposite.   Walk up this lane, past a gated track on your left and with the fields sloping down beyond the hedge on your right.   As the lane bends slightly left, there is a new car park on your left just before the National Trust sign for "Wilkswood" - edged with mainly oaks and beeches. Listed as *Wilceswde* in the Domesday Book, it was held by the wife of Hugh FitzGrip whilst Durand was her tenant.   By the mid-1800s, the property had passed to H J P Bankes of Kingston Lacy and it was given to the National Trust in the bequest of Sir Ralph Bankes, the last of the Bankes' family of Kingston Lacy and Corfe Castle, in 1985.   A few yards past the sign, the lane continues to Wilkswood Farm but this is a "Private Road" and you have to turn off right at the Bridleway-arrowed post onto a shady, stony track with ferns and bracken all around.   Be careful now as there are a couple of side turnings which you must not miss.   As the track bends round to the right to a farm gate and a sloping field, turn off the track onto a narrow path on your left, between bracken and bushes.   Follow the winding path (which is really a Bridleway) for just a few yards until the trees thin out and a path turns off to your right.   Don't go right but keep straight on - but only for a few more steps.   The main path continues straight on but you have to turn off it to the left where you will find a stile in a wire fence with a steep slope on the other side.   Found it? Well done.

Over the stile, carefully negotiate the bracken-covered steps in the steep banked clay hillside and you will suddenly find yourself in the valley floor with beeches overhead and a grass path beneath your feet.   This is a beautifully quiet and pleasant spot, especially with the stream zig-zagging through reeds and bullrushes and under the mossy, stony bridge which leads you to the uphill slope on the other side.   Follow the uphill path along a narrow, stony 'stream bed' and out of Wilkswood over a Footpath-arrowed stile.   You emerge, blinking, onto bracken and teazle-clad slopes of a high heath with odd trees and hawthorn bushes all around.   The electricity pole ahead of you carries a confirmation Footpath arrow which directs you straight on, across left and right paths, and up between bushes onto more of the open downs.

When you meet a wider, rocky, grassy track coming up from your left and heading for a gate in the top RH fence, turn right and follow it up.   It fades before reaching the fence but keep straight up to the stile with the painted yellow arrow and climb over into the next field.   Bear left and follow the LH edge of the hedged field uphill.

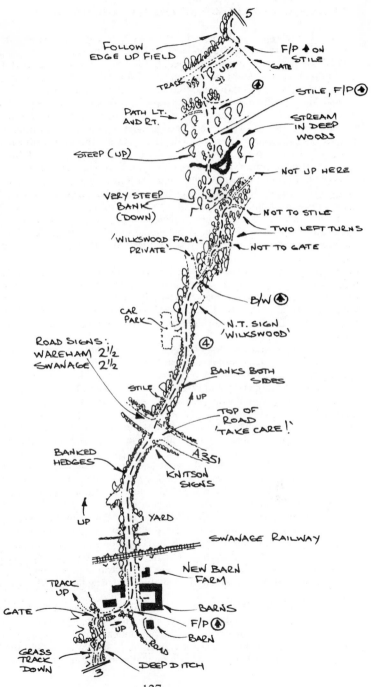

FOLLOW
EDGE UP FIELD

5

F/P ↟ ON
STILE

GATE

TRACK UP

STILE, F/P ⊕

PATH LT.
AND RT.

STREAM
IN DEEP
WOODS

STEEP (UP)

NOT UP HERE

VERY STEEP
BANK
(DOWN)

NOT TO STILE

TWO LEFT TURNS

'WILKSWOOD FARM-
PRIVATE'

NOT TO GATE

B/W ⊕

CAR
PARK

N.T. SIGN
'WILKSWOOD'

ROAD SIGNS:
WAREHAM 2½
SWANAGE 2½

④

BANKS BOTH
SIDES

STILE

↑ UP

TOP OF
ROAD
'TAKE CARE !'

BANKED
HEDGES

A351

KNITSON
SIGNS

↑
UP

YARD

SWANAGE RAILWAY

NEW BARN
FARM

TRACK
UP

BARNS

GATE

UP

F/P ⊕

BARN

GRASS
TRACK
DOWN

ROAD

3

DEEP DITCH

127

STAGE 5

WILKSWOOD AND LEESON FIELDS TO LANGTON HOUSE

ROUTE 1: Right, pay attention.   I lost myself here and I don't want you doing the same.   When you reach the stile and gate half-way up the LH hedge, you will find two Footpath arrows pointing into the next field.   Although there are lovely views straight on towards Ballard Down, Swanage and the Isle of Wight, you don't want to go that way.   Be sure to turn right, following the hedge which borders the top half of the field which you have just left, to the top of this field.   A few yards from the top RH corner, you will find a broken kissing gate without any arrows (unless it's all mended now).   Go through the gate into the next, uphill field and head slightly left up to the top LH corner.   Go through the farm gate and cross the small enclosure with a barn on your left to the next gate.   Through this gate, you will find a painted yellow arrow on the other side of the barn so you have been on the right path.   So, with a big tree on the opposite corner, turn sharp right onto a farm track but only for a few yards.   Then, with a sign "Out of Bounds" on your right, turn left and follow the hedged, stony track uphill to a cross-tracks with Durnford View on the RH corner. Durnford Farm gains its name from its ancient owners, first of whom was William de Durneford.   In the mid-1800s, it belonged, together with Belle View Farm and California Farm, both of which are just off Priests Way, to the Serrell family.

The lane now becomes tarmac with the athletics field of Old Malthouse School over on your left.   Various cottages, sheds and school buildings border the lane until you arrive in Langton Matravers opposite Garfield Cottage.   Turn left and walk down, past St George's First School with its Playing Fields opposite and past Mount Pleasant Lane.   Turn right into Durnford Drove, signposted "Dancing Ledge 1.1/4".

ROUTE 3: Climb over the stone-stepped stile in the far LH corner, adjacent to the stone-walled trees which surround Leeson House.   Earlier the seat of the Clavells of Leston, it was used during World War II as H Q for planning the D-Day invasions. With Churchill, Montgomery and Eisenhower in residence, it's little wonder that gun-posts were erected all around the perimeter.   Bear slightly right across the field, 340 degrees NNW, to find the National Trust "Spyway Farm" sign and climb over the stile into a grass path between two gardens. Follow the path round and go through the gate into a housing estate called "Steppes Hill".   Turn right and walk down to the main road into Langton Matravers.   Originally in two parts, Langton Wallis and Langton Matravers, the two villages gained their names from "long town" and the titles of their ancient lords.   Turn left and pass Manor Farm Cottage and the "Ship Inn" before descending, past a "IX miles from Warehem" stone, to Putlake Farm Centre and W.C. Keep to the pavement, past Crack Lane on your right, and up past "The Hyde" on your left.   The "King's Arms" was built at the end of the 18thC and was long the haunt of quarrymen.   Keep on up, past the Old Rectory, to St George's church of which only the old tower remains following the 1828 restoration - "which lays little claim to Architectural propriety": Hutchins.   The Register goes back to 1670 and John de Mautravers was a patron here in 1322.   The village hall of 1845 stands opposite the church and, just past here, turn left into Durnford Drove and join up with Route 1.

ROUTE 1 with ROUTE 3: Follow Durnford Drove, past the Scout Hut on your right and past East Drove and Gypshayes on your left, to the end where a silver arrow directs you through the gateway onto a climbing tarmac driveway with a stone wall on your left and a sycamore lined ditch on your right.   A gate leads onto the tree-lined drive of Langton House but keep straight on up the, now stony, track.

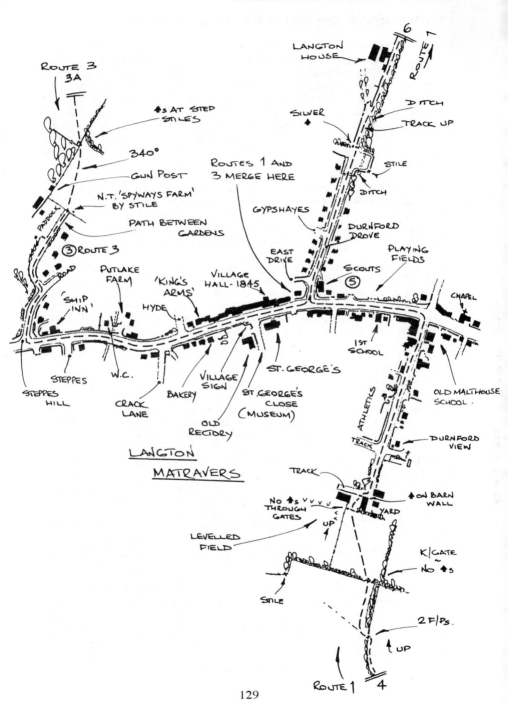

LANGTON HOUSE

ROUTE 3
3A

▲s AT STEP STILES

SILVER

DITCH

TRACK UP

340°

GUN POST

ROUTES 1 AND 3 MERGE HERE

STILE

DITCH

N.T. 'SPYWAYS FARM' BY STILE

GYPSHAYES

DURNFORD DROVE

PLAYING FIELDS

PATH BETWEEN GARDENS

PADDOCK

③ROUTE 3

EAST DRIVE

SCOUTS
⑤

CHAPEL

ROAD

PUTLAKE FARM

'KING'S ARMS'

VILLAGE HALL-1845

'SHIP INN'

HYDE

1ST SCHOOL

STEPPES

W.C.

VILLAGE SIGN

ST. GEORGE'S

ATHLETICS

OLD MALTHOUSE SCHOOL.

STEPPES HILL

BAKERY

ST. GEORGE'S CLOSE (MUSEUM)

CRACK LANE

OLD RECTORY

DURNFORD VIEW

TRACK

LANGTON
MATRAVERS

TRACK

NO ▲s THROUGH GATES

UP

▲ON BARN WALL

YARD

LEVELLED FIELD

K/GATE
NO ▲s

STILE

2 F/Ps.

↑ UP

ROUTE 1   4

ROUTE 1

STAGE 6

LANGTON HOUSE AND PUTLAKE BARN TO SPYWAY FARM

ROUTE 1: Still with Langton House over the high stone wall on your left, keep following the track and ignore the Footpath which turns off right through the bushes before the next Footpath-arrowed gate. Through the gate, the National Trust "Spyway Farm" sign welcomes you to the airy downs before the Coast Path - if you're going that way. Go through the kissing gate by the next gate across your track and keep straight on as the stone wall turns and follows you at a greater distance on your left. There are fine sea views as far as Hurst Point and the Isle of Wight as you begin a long, uppish walk to the end of the LH stone wall. Here you will find a stone labelled "Footpath. Langton and Dancing Ledge" whilst you cross over the "Priests Way" track from Swanage to Worth Matravers.

If you want to go back to Swanage by the Priests Way on Route 4, this is where you turn off and follow Route 4 instructions in the next paragraph - *now* - but, if you're going to Dancing Ledge and the longer coastal Route 1 back, follow the diagonal path across the open grass directly towards the Spyway Farm cottage and stone barn up ahead of you. Now, go straight down to the last paragraph on this page.

ROUTE 4: Turn left onto Priests Way and follow the track to the gate in the far LH corner of this dry-stone walled field of many tracks. Go through the gate and follow the stone wall-entrained, stony track with fine valley views to your left. After the T-junction of tracks, where a path goes right into the field for "Dancing Ledge" (it's not too late to change your mind) the track begins a long, easy descent, passing another "Priests Way" stone on the way to a gate which crosses your route between stone walls and a cluster of sycamores.

Now, turn to Stage 3A and follow the Stage maps from top to bottom instead of the usual bottom to top which you have done until now. From Stage 3A, turn to Stage 2A and 10/1A. This will bring you back to Swanage along Priests Way and over the abandoned stone-mining area with some lovely views as you progress. I had to reverse one of the Routes stages and, unfortunately, Route 4 drew the short straw - mainly because it will be quite easy to find the way back from here.

ROUTE 2: Through the gate and after the "Priests Way. Worth" stone, follow the track uphill between banks, walls and hedges for 1/2 mile, crossing a path which comes from a right track and runs left through a high field to "Dancing Ledge" on the way. Don't go that way as it approaches Dancing Ledge from entirely the wrong direction for our purposes. When you reach another gate across your path, leading into a dry-stone wall enclosed field with tracks all over the place, turn onto the left-bearing, stony track and follow it to Spyway Farm cottage and barns. Here, join up with Route 1 to follow details of the walk, starting below, back along the Coast Path to Swanage.

ROUTE 1 with ROUTE 2: On arrival at Spyway Barn, you will find a kissing gate next to the farm gate leading into the farmyard. Go through and walk past the stone cottage on your left and the large stone barn on your right to the next kissing gate which leads you onto a grass track running across a long, high field to a stone-pillared gate in the dry-stone wall opposite. Go through this gate into another long field with views ahead to the sea but with all other views cut off by slightly higher fields all round. Follow the grass track straight ahead.

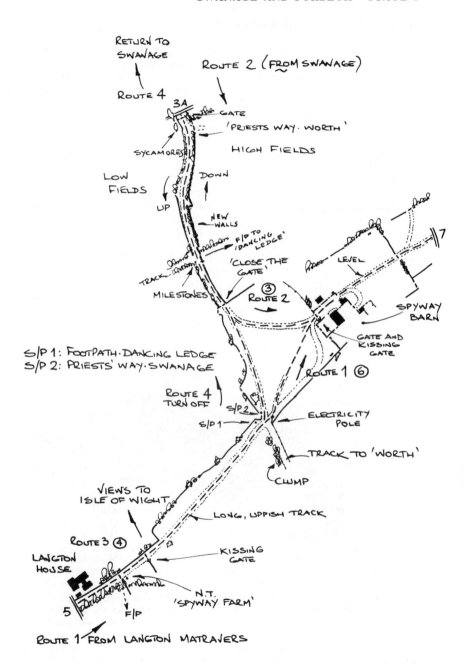

RETURN TO
SWANAGE

ROUTE 2 (FROM SWANAGE)

ROUTE 4

3A

GATE

'PRIESTS WAY · WORTH'

SYCAMORES

HIGH FIELDS

LOW
FIELDS

DOWN

UP

NEW
WALLS

F/P TO
'DANCING
LEDGE'

'CLOSE THE
GATE'

LEVEL

7

TRACK

MILESTONES

③ ROUTE 2

SPYWAY
BARN

GATE AND
KISSING
GATE

S/P 1: FOOTPATH · DANCING LEDGE
S/P 2: PRIESTS' WAY · SWANAGE

ROUTE 1 ⑥

ROUTE 4
TURN OFF

S/P 2

S/P 1

ELECTRICITY
POLE

TRACK TO 'WORTH'

CLUMP

VIEWS TO
ISLE OF WIGHT

LONG, UPPISH TRACK

ROUTE 3 ④

LANGTON
HOUSE

KISSING
GATE

5

F/P

N.T.
'SPYWAY FARM'

ROUTE 1 FROM LANGTON MATRAVERS

STAGE 7

SPYWAY FARM TO BLACKERS HOLE

The track arrives at a kissing gate with a farm gate further across to your right.   Go through the gate to be greeted by a wonderful view and a stone advising the way to "Dancing Ledge".   From here, you want to get to the bottom of the hill where the distant wire fence joins the descending stone wall over on your right.   Begin your descent to the right of the stone, at first on shallow Purbeck stone slabs as steps but then on the steep, natural grassy slopes.   This is a 225 ft drop all at once so enjoy it and don't go too fast.   Arriving at the bottom corner, the Coast Path runs away into the right field past a stone marked "Seacombe and Winspit", two of the most famous sea-cliff quarries in the Isle of Purbeck.   I would really recommend "Purbeck Shop", the fine chronicle of Purbeck quarrymen's' lives up to the year 1930 by one of the most literate of the hardy breed, Eric Benfield.   It will give a much clearer appreciation of the difficulties, physical and economical, of working the Purbeck stone quarries and underground mines and how life-long friends shared the dangers and the companionship of their calling.   The landscape of these clifftops and cliff faces bears testimony to the long struggle to win stone from the Purbeck hills.

For a perfect example of a cliff quarry and the hazardous ship-loading quays utilised by these brave men, climb over one of the stiles, go down the rock steps to Dancing Ledge and try to imagine the efforts needed to hew stone from these cliff faces.   It is a wonderful spot now, frequented by cliff climbers, divers, geologists, bird-watchers and young lads jumping - as others have for years before them - from the scarily high cliffs above the caves into the clear deep waters below.

Dancing Ledge, Purbeck

Return to the twin stiles above the climbing cliffs and turn right to follow the Coast Path along the top, wire fence.   It is about 2.1/2 miles to Durlston Country Park and you begin by walking up, then down, then up, then down and across a boggy bit, then down some more and up steeply to the first stile at the end of a dry-stone wall where a higher path leads to Durlston.   As the Coast Path is a series of ups and downs over the now grass-covered workings and spoil from the mines, I refuse point blank to note any more inclines.   In fact, I'll just tell you that you have two more stiles on this Stage so, keep heading East and enjoy the views, the sea breezes and the cries of the gulls.   Oh, the rocky headland which you will see close by as you reach the end of this Stage is Blackers Hole.

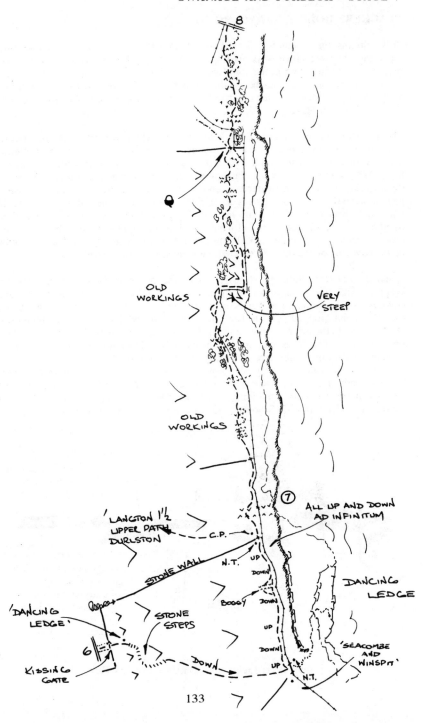

8

OLD
WORKINGS

VERY
STEEP

OLD
WORKINGS

⑦ ALL UP AND DOWN
AD INFINITUM

'LANGTON 1½
UPPER PATH
DURLSTON   C.P.

N.T.   UP
DOWN   DANCING
LEDGE

STONE WALL

BOGGY   DOWN

'DANCING
LEDGE'   STONE
STEPS   UP

6   DOWN
DOWN   'SEACOMBE
AND
WINSPIT'

KISSING
GATE   DOWN   UP
N.T.

133

STAGE 8

BLACKERS HOLE TO ANVIL POINT

Still enjoying the undulating Coast Path, go past the two stiles in the adjacent LH
fence with the steel lattice-work mast by the side of the path between the two. You
may be wondering what is the significance of these masts. They don't have any
cables or lights or aerials attached to them so what could be their purpose? You may
know already but don't say anything and, when the others have had time to consider
it, I'll tell you on Stage 9.

The next stile delivers you to "Belle Vue" through which you are sheltered from the
clifftops by a wire fence - or is it the nesting gulls who are being sheltered?
Anyway, three fields later you leave "Belle Vue" over the last stile which brings you
into "Durlston Country Park". The narrow path now ascends to join a wider, stony,
dusty or claggy clay path (depending upon the current weather). Enjoy this easier
path between the banked LH wire fence and the scrub and bushes above the RH cliffs
until, up to four lanes wide, it arrives on the grassy downs West of the Anvil Point
lighthouse. By all means, go and have a look at the lighthouse but the Coast Path
descends from thence to the rocks below the lighthouse, requiring a difficult scramble
up the bare cliff on the other side. Let's go the easier way - so follow me.

When the LH fence runs out, bear left over the greensward, uphill slightly and
keeping a high, rocky knoll to your right. Passing several close paths which come
down from the stiles and gates in the stone wall up on the ridge to your left, go up and
over the rabbit-cropped grass to find the tarmac lane which serves the lighthouse.
Step down onto the drive, turn left and go through the gates with the "Butterfly Trail
Ends" notice. This leads you, between hawthorn and blackthorn bushes to a painted,
stone-walled bridge which crosses a deep, bush-filled gully on its way to the low
rocks below the sealed-off Tilly Whim quarry. Keep following the drive round and
begin a steady uphill climb with good views down to Tilly Whim and the cliff path
which you are temporarily avoiding. By the way, Tilly was the name of a local
quarryman and Whim is the wooden crane used for loading the stone blocks.

Anvil Point Lighthouse, Durslton Country Park

134

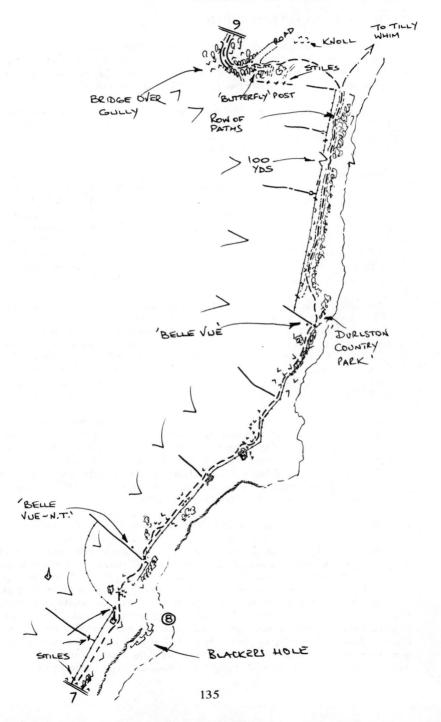

9

ROAD

KNOLL

TO TILLY
WHIM

STILES

BRIDGE OVER
GULLY

'BUTTERFLY' POST

ROW OF
PATHS

100
YDS

'BELLE VUE'

'DURLSTON
COUNTRY
PARK'

'BELLE
VUE~N.T.'

STILES

⑧

BLACKERS HOLE

7

135

STAGE 9

ANVIL POINT TO PEVERIL DOWN

Continuing up the tarmac road, now between high banks, you soon arrive at a reconstructed mine entrance showing the horse-powered winch which drew the huge blocks of stone from the deep workings into the first light they had seen since the Jurassic period.   This is just like the photograph on the cover of "Purbeck Shop".

Turning around and facing the sea, you will notice two more lattice-work masts and it is just over a mile since you saw the other two.   That's it exactly.   They are marker posts indicating a measured *nautical* mile and used by many ships which frequented Portland Harbour just along the coast, West from here.

To continue, follow the road up to the top gate and go through onto the old road where about 10 cars could park before the advent of the Country Park and its vast parking facilities.   The gap in the short section of stone wall on your left leads to the Park Centre and Toilets, either of which may be useful.   Keep along this level roadway with shady trees on your right until you pass one of Mr Burt's bollards from London and reach a junction of car park roads and some steps down through the RH trees to "Coast Path. Tilly Whim".   Keep to the pavement alongside the stone wall whilst all that vehicular commotion takes place to your left and go down a couple of steps onto the top of the lane which leads down to Durlston Castle on your right.

Cross this lane and go into the narrow, stone-walled path opposite.   This brings you to a T-junction with a wider, gravel path which comes up from "Tilly Whim and Lighthouse".   Turn left and begin an easy stroll through trees on the wide path, past the first left path to "Car Park and Park Centre".   You are now on the Victorian and Woodland Trail from Durlston with glimpses through the RH trees of Durlston Bay whilst better views can be enjoyed from any of the viewpoint seats above the bay as you progress.   A high wire fence on your left runs out at Solent Road, a strangely wide yet hardly important bit of road which runs away through a gate on your left.

The trees around you are mainly beeches, sycamores and chestnuts as the path descends between stone walls and bears right and left, past bench spots and good views of the bay, into a deeply wooded section with narrower paths.   Keep to the main path following the clifftops, across a wooden bridge over a stream with harts-tongue ferns proliferating, and around a right bend with a stone-built seat.   This is a gift to Dorset County Council from Costa Mesa, California on the 200th anniversary of the founding of the U.S.A. - dated 6th December 1976.

Keep going round, past the patch of floor tiles which are all that remain from a house which plummeted into the sea during one of the Durslton Bay landslips.   This is a particularly unstable area with two major faults and it seems an odd place to build multi-storey blocks of flats, especially the "Durlston Cliff" block which you will see at the top of the steps as you reach Belle Vue Road.   Turn right and follow the high stone wall around and through the gate onto Peveril Down, keeping to the gravel path until you reach a couple of seats behind the RH bushes.   There are lovely views from here but the path has run out so bear left and begin an angular descent of the Downs.   Past the fenced gardens of the white-painted Uplands, aim generally for the far, bottom LH corner below the last chestnut tree.   A good guide is the stone wall coming down from the hill on your left.   You want to arrive at the farthest, lowest end of this wall.   Now turn to the penultimate paragraph of Stage 10/1A on the next page.

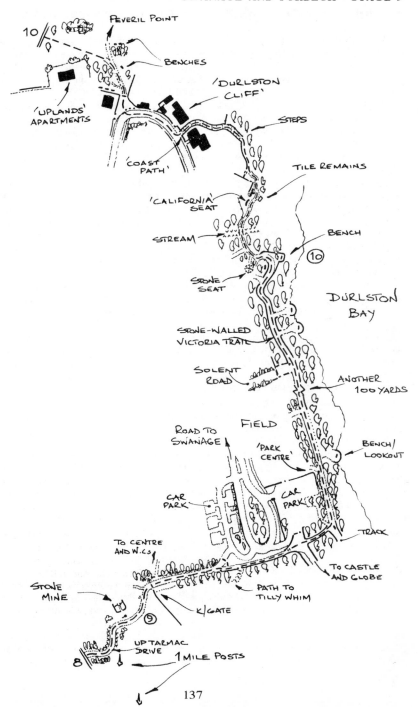

PEVERIL POINT

BENCHES

'DURLSTON CLIFF'

'UPLANDS' APARTMENTS

STEPS

TILE REMAINS

'COAST PATH'

'CALIFORNIA' SEAT

STREAM

BENCH

(10)

STONE SEAT

DURLSTON BAY

STONE-WALLED VICTORIA TRAIL

SOLENT ROAD

ANOTHER 100 YARDS

FIELD

ROAD TO SWANAGE

'PARK CENTRE'

BENCH/ LOOKOUT

CAR PARK

CAR PARK

TRACK

TO CENTRE AND W.Cs

TO CASTLE AND GLOBE

STONE MINE

PATH TO TILLY WHIM

K/GATE

(9)

UP TARMAC DRIVE

1 MILE POSTS

8

137

STAGE 10/1A

PEVERIL DOWN TO SWANAGE/SWANAGE TO TOWNSEND HEIGHTS

ROUTE 2 DEPARTURE: From the Tourist Information Centre on the seafront, turn and walk towards the town as far as the granite column with the cannon balls on top. This commemorates a battle "fought with the Danes in Swanage Bay AD 877" but, in that same year, part of the Danish Army that had overwintered in Wareham sailed from Wareham and "a violent storm and their ignorance of the coast carried them onto Peveril Point where 120 were lost": Hutchins. Walk behind the Mowlem Theatre and follow the sea wall past the Victorian "Parade" with its ornate cast-iron lamp standards from Hanover Square, London. Then turn right between the Parade end and the large W.C. block. This brings you to "The Square" where you turn right and cross over the pedestrian crossing and continue walking right into High Street.

Keep straight on past "The Anchor" on your right and the "Red Lion" on your left. Further up, on the right, stands the Town Hall. This building was erected in 1882 and it incorporates the hugely ornate front from the Mercers' Hall, London which was designed by Edward Jarman after the Great Fire of London in 1666. Shortly after the Town Hall, there is a plaque where John Wesley stayed in October 1774. Sadly, the cottage was destroyed in World War II. The high-walled building on your left is Purbeck House, built in the late 19thC by George Burt, nephew of John Mowlem. It was until recently a convent but is now a hotel, in the grounds of which are several stone carvings and architectural fragments which Mr Burt shipped back from London as ballast in his stone delivery ships. When you pass the Methodist Church, turn left up the tarmac passageway with the Social Services building on your right.

High stone walls bring you onto a bend in Queen's Road with plenty of shady trees and fine houses behind low stone walls. Keep on up the hill, passing the Cottage Hospital over on your right and crossing the T-junction where the road now becomes Bon Accord Road. Past Atlantic Road on your right, take the next right Russell Avenue with the "Public Footpath" sign on the corner. A short distance up on your right, turn into "Rough Height" at another "Footpath" sign and follow the lane, shortly turning to stony grass, through a gate into an open, grassy area with a stone cottage on your left and a panoramic view over Swanage Bay on your right. As the track runs out around the back of the cottage, follow the rough path into bushes and between two slotted stone posts to reach a crossing tarmac lane. Zig-zag lt/rt across the lane to a kissing gate up the opposite bank with "Dorset Wildlife Trust Nature Reserve" and "Footpath" signs. Paths through here are many and varied but, if you ignore all side paths and follow the instructions, you shouldn't get lost. Through scrub and bushes, go up wooden steps or keep to the right of a deep clump - they both meet on the other side. Then go round to the right of the next deep clump where you will meet a rising wire fence with a superb view to Ballard Down. From here, keep straight on alongside the fence to find a Footpath arrow on its end post.

ROUTE 1 and 2 RETURNS: At the bottom corner, go down the stone steps, turn left and leave Broad Road into Seymer Road. Turn down towards the sea and stroll back to the start by following the stone sea wall past the Amusements, the W.C block and along the "Parade" to the Mowlem Theatre from where you can see the T.I.C.

ROUTE 4 RETURN: From the fence post with the Footpath arrow, follow Stage 10/1A from top to bottom and follow the text, in reverse. Thanks for following the Route from Putlake Barn in reverse. Do a coastal Route next time - it'll be easier.

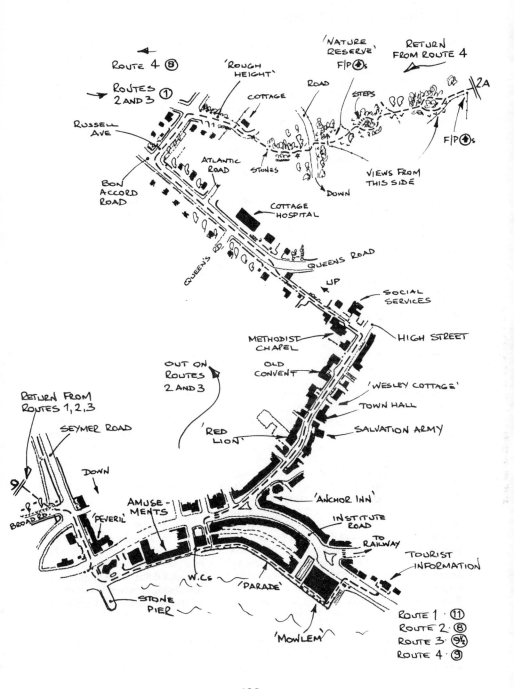

STAGE 2A

TOWNSEND HEIGHTS TO BELLE VIEW LANE

ROUTE 2: Over a ridge and past a quarry hole on your right, you reach a path which comes up from the right through some scattered sycamores.   Turn left and join this path as it runs uphill, bearing a little left and passing through bushes before emerging into a deep gully.   At the top of this gully, the path keeps straight on up towards a kissing gate on the horizon but *don't follow it.*   Instead, turn sharp right, around more bushes, to find a grassy path running along the old, quarried slopes with a pair of raised grassy platforms up on your left (one fenced).   Go past a solitary post in the middle of the path and aim for the next post, about 50 yards away in the same direction.   Keep ignoring all paths which run off in any direction and aim for some caravans which appear beyond bushes straight ahead.   Go through the twin half-gates, signed "Townsend Nature Reserve", out onto a right-to-left uphill tarmac lane.

Turn down the lane and go over the Footpath-arrowed stile in the wire fence just before two sycamore trees.   You are now in Hoburne Park and the arrow directs you down to the right.   Follow the tarmac roadway around a left-sweeping bend and descend to a main driveway.   Zig-zag down and up, rt/lt past No 104 on the far RH corner, and then keep to the road past a LH turn.   Now, descend to zig-zag down and up again, rt/lt across another main driveway with No 88 on the LH corner.   Still maintaining your generally Western direction along the slope, walk up the road, past a LH branch to "No 82 No Footpath", and begin a descent to your right.   Don't go very far though.   With a caravan on either side of the downhill drive, turn instantly left to a Footpath-arrowed stile as trees and bushes line the LH verge.

Stile arrows point left and right as you climb over onto a wide greensward where tents are pitched but the RH path only runs down to the town.   The LH Footpath, which starts at the next stile on the LH bank, should lead you in an arc to the far end of this second caravan park but it is out of service - unless it's been reinstated by now.   I've checked with the Site Manager of Priestsway Holiday Park and been advised to stay on the grassy shelf because "Everybody goes that way".   So keep straight on, past two water tanks on your left and with a steep drop into the caravan area on your right, until you arrive (past the returning, defunct stile from the arcing path) onto another right-to-left rising tarmac lane.

Uphill, the road leads to California Farm and, momentarily, this is your direction. 15 yards up the hill, a Coast Path stone stands against the RH bushy verge.   Turn right here in the "Footpath" direction and go up the rocky steps through the scrub to a Footpath-arrowed stile.   Over this stile, you are in a widening field with a wire fence on your left and a stone wall overlooking extensive valley views on your right.   A strange semi-circular bank faces you for the full width of the field.   Go either side of this and then aim for the far RH corner of the field where you will find a gate in the RH stone wall before a low, stone barn.   Go through the gate into the lower field beyond and turn sharp left after a short, stone-walled gully.   Just past the stone barn, there is a gate which leads out onto a stony track leading from "Belle Vue Farm - Private Road" down on the right.   Cross over the track to the opposite field and climb over the stile next to a gate with a Priests Way sign for "Worth 3" and "Coast 1".

ROUTE 4: Start at the top of Stage 2A and follow it downwards as you just did with Stage 3A.   Then turn to Stage 1A for the last leg across the rest of the quarry grounds and through Swanage.   You'll find the text interesting on Stage 1A - but upside-down.

SWANAGE AND PURBECK - STAGE 2A

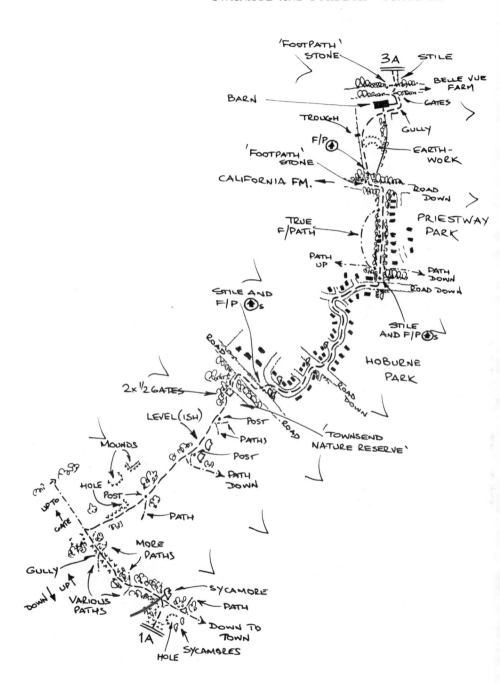

BELLE VUE LANE TO PUTLAKE BARN AND LEESON FIELDS

ROUTE 2: Follow the RH wire fence across two fields, crossing a farm track at a complex of gates and fence junctions on the way. Then go through the gate in a bush-covered stone wall onto a narrower, bushed path. Shortly, the path widens out into an undulating farm track with a low fence on your left with a gateway below you.

In deeper trees and bushes, you arrive at a stone wall with a stone step-stile and a gate. Over the stile, you are in an open area with a track turning off to your right for "Herston 3/4" and your way is confirmed as "Priests Way". Keep straight on, past the derelict brick cottage over the LH stone wall. Go over another stone step-stile next to another gate onto an old, broken tarmac track which soon breaks up completely into grass and stones. A gate opens up to your left into an area of barns behind the bushes but keep straight on with bushes lining the track on both sides. After a few more yards, you reach another division of tracks with the most obvious one going straight ahead - to "Gully 1/4". *Don't follow it* but turn left past the LH corner gate onto a track which the Priests Way stone indicates for "Worth 2.1/2".

This track with the stone wall on its right heads up to "South Barn" which has been converted into a most desirable dwelling surrounded by stone walls. The official Path actually heads across to the gate in the stone wall over on your left, well away from the house, and then doubles back to lead right around the far side of the house. Common usage seems to favour the more obvious track which hugs the wall around the LH side of the house and turns right between the back of the house and the field wall. So, behind the house, follow the LH field wall, past a gate, down to another gate which leads you out of this field. A stone which is set into the wall by the side of the gate confirms the direction for "Priests Way. Langton".

Go through the gate, walk past the turning to the left and go down to the bending stony track in front of you. Now you have to decide whether to keep straight on along Priests Way to Spyway Barn or to turn off across the fields to visit the quarrymen's village of Langton Matravers, passing Leeson House, the Ship Inn, the Kings Arms and St George's church on the way before arriving at Spyway Barn.

Straight on is Route 2 and the diversion is Route 3 so choose your directions now.

ROUTE 2: Follow the stony track with a long, low field over the wire fence on your right, past the gated and wood-fenced Putlake Barn and into a shadier section of walled and fenced track on a left bend.

ROUTE 3: Cross the track immediately and climb over the stile into the long. low field over the wire fence. Now, take aim across the low, boggy centre of the field to find a stile in the far LH wall and hedge. To assist, the stile is about 100 yards left of the solitary, but large, sycamore tree by the far RH wall. - or 320 degrees NW. Reaching the stile, climb over and bend a little more right (340 degrees NNW) and aim for a stile in the far corner of the next field, near the LH end of the wood.

ROUTE 4: Start at the top of Stage 3A and follow it downwards. As you're now an expert in following these maps, this is your chance to show those who are using this same map as Route 2 (the right way round) that you can do it standing on your head. Then follow Stages 2A and 1A to find your way through the old quarries to Swanage.

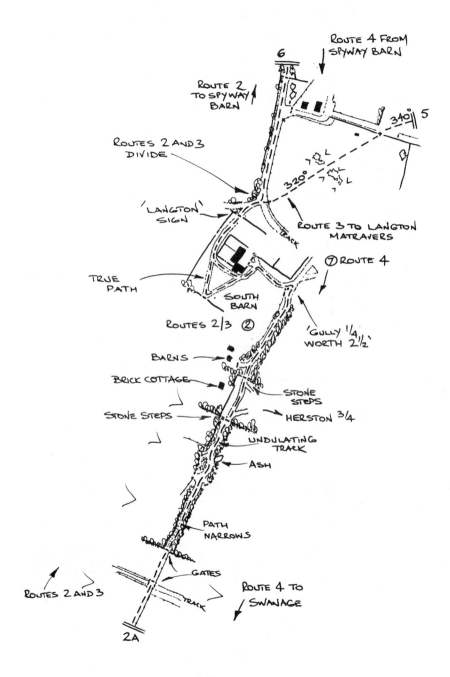

ROUTE 4 FROM
SPYWAY BARN

6

ROUTE 2
TO SPYWAY
BARN

340° 5

ROUTES 2 AND 3
DIVIDE

320°

L

L

L

ROUTE 3 TO LANGTON
MATRAVERS

'LANGTON'
SIGN

TRACK

⑦ ROUTE 4

TRUE
PATH

SOUTH
BARN

ROUTES 2/3 ②

'GULLY ¼
WORTH 2½'

BARNS

BRICK COTTAGE

STONE
STEPS

STONE STEPS

HERSTON ¾

UNDULATING
TRACK

ASH

PATH
NARROWS

GATES

ROUTES 2 AND 3

TRACK

ROUTE 4 TO
SWANAGE

2A

IN CONCLUSION

Whilst looking through the finished drawings and maps in this book, memories of the intimate exploration of this loveliest of English counties flood back into my head. I'm glad I was persuaded to publish a selection of special circular walks even though I had originally set out to design a few brand new long-distance paths for the ramblers of Dorset. I suppose it was the desire to show my compatriots that Dorset has much more than the beautiful coastline that is so beloved of guide book and calendar publishers. I became so enamoured of the hidden parts of inland Dorset whilst preparing the long walks which are listed behind the title page that, far from being an interval between arranging more of these long walks, the preparation of these day and half-day walks proved to be enormously rewarding.

I'd never walked around the Isle of Portland before I came to write this book and, during the time of my exploration of this unique 'island', I was enchanted by the magnificent, rugged cliffs, the grey Portland stone buildings and cottages, the superb sea views and the vast skies. The routes from Swanage display an entirely different coastline with softer valleys and more mellow stone buildings but with the same high cliffs and magnificent views. Moving inland, the beautiful Winterborne villages in their warm valley with high, enclosing woods were a revelation with enchanting cottages and a unique church close to an ancient tithe barn and manor house. The country South of Sherborne epitomises all that is best about the villages, farms and stately homes of the Blackmore Vale whilst the Stour River valley walk North of Sturminster Newton visits some favourite villages and water mills. The extended walks around Chettle, Eastbury and Farnham explore some of the less visited areas of the Cranborne Chase with super long distance views from the high downs and visits to some really beautiful churches and fine houses.

In short, this book will lead you to some sublime countryside which will provide you with memories that you will cherish for many years to come.

ACKNOWLEDGMENTS

Thanks to my wife Janet for coming with me on some of these new walks   Often, it's not until I've undertaken the walks as fun days out rather than days of working, sketching and writing that I really appreciate how lovely they really are.   On the working days, Jan's packed lunches have provided a feast in the open air, sometimes on hot, sun-drenched days and sometimes sheltering under much-appreciated trees.

Here, may I acknowledge the shelter provided by trees of all sorts, sometimes giving extra oxygen and respite from the blazing sun and sometimes providing shelter from opened heavens.   Our unofficial survey suggests that maple trees are the best umbrellas, followed by beech and oak with coppiced hazel coming way down the list.

Thanks again to everybody at the Lansdowne Reference Library in Bournemouth and in the Rights of Way Section at Dorchester.

Now, long overdue, may I thank dear old A W Wainwright for inspiring me to look at Dorset in much the same way as he looked at his beloved Lake District.   He said "The map of England is an oyster very rich in pearls.   Plan your own marathon and do something never done before, something you will enjoy, a route that will take you to places often read about but never yet seen, unhampered by human beings en bloc". I'm delighted to be able to follow his example - albeit falteringly.

BIBLIOGRAPHY

History and Antiquities of the County of Dorset: Rev John Hutchins 1861- 64 edition
Inventory of Historical Monuments in the County of Dorset: H.M.S.O. 1970
Dorset Churches: Sir Owen Morshead: Dorset Historic Churches Trust 1976
The Place Names of Dorset - Parts 2 and 3: A D Mills of the English Place Names
          Society - Edited by K Cameron.
Portrait of Dorset: Ralph Wightman: Robert Hale
Inside Dorset: Monica Hutchings 1964
Geology Explained in Dorset: John W Perkins: David and Charles
Geology and Scenery in England and Wales: A E Truman: Pelican Books
The Island and Royal Manor of Portland 1750 - 1851: J H Bettey, University of
Bristol 1970
Purbeck Shop: Eric Benfield: Ensign Publications
Cranborne Chase: Desmond Hawkins: Victor Gollancz 1980
A Chronicle of Cranborne and Cranborne Chase: T W Wake Smart 1841
The Domesday Book: Edited by Thomas Hinde: Guild Publishing

INDEX

Prospect Farm, Swanage 122
Pulpit Inn, Portland 14
Putlake Barn, Purbeck 130,138,142
Putlake Farm, Langton Matravers 128

Quarleston Farm, W/B Stickland 106,108
Quarry Lane, Long Burton 60,62
Queen's Road, Swanage 138

Raleigh, Sir Walter 56,74
Red Lion, Swanage 138
Reforne, Easton 10
Rempston, Robert 122
Rights of Way Act 1990 3
Rixon, Sturminster Newton 48,50
Road Lane Farm, Colber 34
Roger de Caen, Bishop 56
Roger, Bishop of Salisbury 56
Rose and Crown, Long Burton 62
Rufus Castle, Portland 18,20
Rushay 36
Russell Avenue, Swanage 138
Ryall's Farm, Bishops Down 66

School Lane, Tarrant Gunville 80,84
Seacombe, Purbeck 132
Serrell family 128
Seymer Road, Swanage 138
Sheat Quarry, Portland 18
Sherborne 52
  New Castle 56,72,74
  Old Castle 56
Ship Inn, Langton Matravers 128,142
Shire Horse, W/borne Stickland 106
Solent Road, Durlston 136
Somerset, Earl of 74
South Barn, Purbeck 142
South Farm, Farnham 88
Southwell, Portland 12
Spring Lane, Long Burton 62
Spyway Farm 128,130,132,142
Square, Swanage 138
St Aldhelm's Head 22
St Katherine's Chapel, Haydon 72
St Mary's Abbey, Shaftesbury 42
St Mary's Abbey, Sherborne 56
Stalbridge 30,34
Stalbridge Lane 34,36
Steppes Hill, Langton Matravers 128
Stone Lodge, M/Abbas 100,102,114
Stopes, Dr Marie 12,22
Stour, River 34,40,44
Straits, Easton 10,20

Sturminster Mill 34
Sturminster Newton 48,50
Sturt, Sir Anthony 82
Suckthumb Quarry, Portland 18
Sylvan Row, Milton Abbas 100
Swanage 116,124,130,138
Swan Inn, Sturminster Newton 30

Tarrant Gunville 80,84,92,94
Thickthorn Long Barrow 82
Thurstan, Bishop of Sherborne 56
Tilly Whim, Durlston 132
Tout Quarry, Portland 26
Townsend Heights, Swanage 138,140
Trade Quarries 28

Valley View Farm, W/B Stickland 106
Vanbrugh, John 80
Verne Prison, Portland 26
Victoria Avenue, Swanage 120
Victoria Hotel, Swanage 120
Vincents Close, Allweston 70

Wakeham, Portland 20,22
Wareham 126,138
Waycroft Quarry, Portland 24
Weares, East and West 12,22,24
Wedgwood, Josiah 94
  Thomas 94
Wenlock 72
Wesley, John 138
West, John 86
West Bay, Portland 28
West Cliff, Portland 18
West Hall, Long Burton 62,64,68
West Hill A3030 58
West Street, W/borne Stickland 106
Weston, Portland 12
Weymouth 14,24,28
Weymouth, Thomas Viscount 72
Whatcombe Common 110
  Wood 114
White Horse, Hinton St Mary 42
Wilkswood 126,128
Windmill Knap, Knitson 124,126
Wingfield-Digby, F J B 74
Winspit, Purbeck 132
Winterborne Clenston 106,108
  Manor House 108
Winterborne Houghton 102,104
Winterborne Stickland 106
Wood Lane, Hinton St Mary 40
Wyatt, James 20